Contemporary's

WORD POWER

Spelling and Vocabulary in Context

Introductory

 McGraw Hill **Wright Group**

Acknowledgments

"D'Nealian® Alphabets and Numbers" from D'NEALIAN HANDWRITING, 2nd Edition, by Donald Neal Thurber, Copyright © 1987, 1991 by Scott Foresman and Company, Glenview Illinois. Reprinted by permission of Scott Foresman-Addison Wesley.

Series Developer
Phil LeFaivre
    Cottage Communications
    Sandwich, Massachusetts

Series Reviewer
Joan Loncich
    Instructor, Adult Basic Education
    Barnstable Community Schools
    Hyannis, Massachusetts

ISBN: 0-8092-0835-0

Send all inquiries to:
Wright Group/McGraw-Hill
130 East Randolph Street, Suite 400
Chicago, Illinois 60601

Printed in the United States of America.

15 14 13 12 11 10 09 RRH 20 19 18 17 16 15 14 13

The **McGraw·Hill** Companies

Word Power
Table of Contents

To the Teacher

Goals of the Series

Word Power provides the mature learner with a systematic program of instruction for reading, writing, and spelling the words needed on the job, at home, and in the community. The vocabulary is arranged thematically at appropriate levels of difficulty and presented in meaningful contexts.

Key Features

1. Word Power *provides instruction at five levels of difficulty, so you can select the book that precisely fits your students' needs.*

   Each of the five *Word Power* books is keyed to a level of the *Tests of Adult Basic Education*, Forms 7 and 8. *Word Power Introductory* correlates with Level L. *Word Power Intermediate 1* and *Intermediate 2* are tied to TABE levels E and M. *Advanced 1* and *Advanced 2* match levels D and A. The four upper-level books offer a pre-test to confirm appropriateness of level and to provide a comparison for post-test purposes.

2. *Words are presented in meaningful contexts. Students immediately see the importance of what they are studying and become motivated to complete the work successfully.*

   Units in the four upper level books are keyed to one of six Comprehensive Adult Student Assessment System (CASAS) Life Skills Competencies: Consumer Economics, Health, Employment, Community Resources, Government and Law, and Learning to Learn.

3. *The skills of reading, writing, and spelling are synchronized to facilitate learning and build a portfolio of successful work.*

   Once students have analyzed the meaning and spelling of the words, they can apply what they have learned in a practical writing and proofreading exercise. A number of the letters, announcements, or similar realistic messages that students write can be mailed or kept in a portfolio of each student's work.

4. *Regular review tests in standardized testing formats allow you to monitor progress while familiarizing your students with the testing strategies they will find in typical GED exams and tests of adult basic skills.*

   Every four-lesson unit concludes with a two-page review test. It checks each student's progress in mastering the meaning and spelling of the words. The testing formats match those used by the TABE.

5. *The easy-to-use format and a Mini-Dictionary at the four upper levels empower students to take control of their learning and work with a high degree of independence.*

   Each lesson follows a sequence through four key stages of learning, which are described on page 7. Students can work independently and progress at their own rate.

6. *The important* Introductory *book provides basic instruction in the key phonetic principles and mechanics skills in a meaningful, adult context.*

   Unlike most programs for mature learners, *Word Power* provides instruction in the basic principles of sounds and letters, and it accomplishes this through high interest, mature content.

Using the Introductory Book

Like all the books in this series, the *Introductory* book consists of twenty-four lessons. After each unit of four lessons, a review test checks students' progress. Each of the twenty-four lessons is divided into four one-page parts that focus on individual steps in the learning process. Depending on your students and your instructional time block, one or more parts or an entire lesson might constitute a class session.

The first four lessons systematically guide students through the sound-letter associations represented by the consonants. The next sixteen lessons focus on a key spelling principle and begin the study of words. These lessons organize words of high utility into lists and exercises designed to facilitate the recognition and application of the principle. The word lists in the final four lessons focus on certain content areas, a strategy followed in the remaining books of the series.

This *Introductory* book is intended for beginning readers. Although the reading level has been kept at the lowest possible level, some students may be unable to read and understand the directions without help. One practical strategy is to identify such students and to work with them as a group, reading the directions aloud to them as they follow along.

This may be an especially useful strategy in the first unit, where students identify and name pictures and begin to associate letters with certain sounds. It is equally important that students accurately identify the pictures and pronounce the names clearly. In such

situations, there is no substitute for the teacher's personal guidance.

The optional Getting Ready material on pages 8 and 9 provides a quick check of visual discrimination skills. Students working at the most basic levels should complete these pages before moving into the regular lesson sequence.

In addition, it is strongly suggested that you review with students the models of manuscript and cursive handwriting on page 122 and the consonant and vowel chart on page 123. Students should be familiar with the letters of the alphabet and be able to differentiate vowels and consonants before beginning the first lesson.

The instructions for completing each part of a lesson are clearly stated and could be performed by many students with a high degree of independence. You may prefer to have students check their own work using the Answer Key on pages 124 through 128. They can record the number correct in the space provided at the bottom of most lesson pages.

The end of the book provides an alphabetical list of all the vocabulary taught in the lessons. It also includes a Personal Word List so that students can record words they learn in this book, at work, at home, or in the community.

As you can see, *Word Power* is an effective and practical tool for addressing the needs of a wide variety of adult learners. We feel confident that *Word Power* will make a significant contribution to your vital work as a teacher.

Breaking Down a Lesson

Beginning with Lesson 5, each lesson progresses through the following stages of instruction:

A Check the Meaning

Here students read the words and infer their meanings by trying out and eventually placing them in a blank space in one of the sentences provided on the page.

B Study the Spelling

This page contains a variety of exercises designed to focus attention on the letters and word parts that make up the spelling of each word.

C Build Your Skills

In this part, a phonetic principle or mechanical skill is stated simply and illustrated with examples. Through a series of exercises, the principle is extended to many words.

D Proofread and Write

A lesson concludes by having students apply what they have learned in an authentic writing and proofreading situation. First students proofread and correct mistakes in a thematic writing model. This activity is followed by a structured writing assignment modeled on the format they have just proofread. Students finish by proofreading and correcting their own work.

Getting Ready

Matching Letters

Look at the letter in the box. Circle the letter that is the same. The first one is done for you.

1. **d**   c   (d)   o   1

2. **m**   x   m   k   n

3. **S**   R   G   S   F

4. **p**   p   q   d   y

5. **v**   z   u   a   v

6. **L**   I   L   B   T

7. **W**   P   Z   W   M

8. **q**   y   q   j   e

9. **c**   k   o   s   c

10. **k**   f   h   k   a

Matching Letters and Words

Look at the word in the box. Circle the word that is the same. The first one is done for you.

11.	**dog**	fog	(dog)	rag	pig
12.	help	held	keep	melt	help
13.	pat	cat	pit	pat	bat
14.	**snow**	**snow**	**grow**	**show**	**blow**
15.	*ring*	*sing*	*wing*	*ring*	*rung*
16.	**Fun**	Sun	Fur	Run	Fun
17.	**won**	**ton**	**now**	**won**	**win**
18.	care	fare	care	cape	dare
19.	**FISH**	**FISH**	**DISH**	**FILM**	**SHIP**
20.	saw	was	sew	sat	saw

Sounds and Letters: *S, M, T, P, N*

Ⓐ Match the Sounds

Name the first picture. Listen to the first sound and note the letter.
Circle the picture with the same first sound. The first one is done for you.

1.

2.

3.

4.

5.

Score: / 5

ⓑ Match the Sounds and Letters

Name the word for each picture. Circle the letter that begins the word.

1.   s   m   t   p   n

2.   s   m   t   p   n

3.   s   m   t   p   n

4.   s   m   t   p   n

5.   s   m   t   p   n

Name the word for each picture. Circle the letter that ends the word.

6.   s   m   t   p   n

7.   s   m   t   p   n

8.   s   m   t   p   n

9.   s   m   t   p   n

10.   s   m   t   p   n

Ⓒ Spell the Sounds

Name the word for each picture. Write the first letter in the word. Then write the word. The first one is done for you.

1. __p__ in   _____pin_____

2. ___un   _____

3. ___an   _____

4. ___ail   _____

5. **10** ___en   _____

6. ___ree   _____

7. ___aw   _____

8. **9** ___ine   _____

9. ___outh   _____

10.  ___izza   _____

Score: /10

D Spell the Sounds

Name the word for each picture. Write the last letter in the word. Then write the word.

1. ma___   _____

2. ca___   _____

3. bu___   _____

4. fa___   _____

5. dru___   _____

6. ca___   _____

7. ne___   _____

8. ca___   _____

9. bar___   _____

10. plu___   _____

Score: ___/10

Lesson 1: Sounds and Letters: *S, M, T, P, N* 13

Sounds and Letters: *L, K, R, B, J*

Ⓐ Match the Sounds

Name the first picture. Listen to the first sound and note the letter.
Circle the picture with the same first sound. The first one is done for you.

1.

2.

3.

4.

5.

Score: /5

Name the word for each picture. Circle the letter that begins the word.

1.    l   k   r   b   j

2.   l   k   r   b   j

3.   l   k   r   b   j

4.   l   k   r   b   j

5.   l   k   r   b   j

Name the word for each picture. Circle the letter that ends the word.

6.   l   k   r   b   j

7.   l   k   r   b   j

8.   l   k   r   b   j

9.   l   k   r   b   j

10.   l   k   r   b   j

Score: ☐/10   **Lesson 2:** Sounds and Letters: *L, K, R, B, J* ⑮

© Spell the Sounds

Name the word for each picture. Write the first letter in the word. Then write the word.

1. ___eg _____

2. ___ing _____

3. ___ird _____

4. ___ite _____

5.  ___et _____

6. ___ook _____

7.  ___ips _____

8. ___ope _____

9.  ___acks _____

10. ___ing _____

Score: ⟋ 10

D Spell the Sounds

Name the word for each picture. Write the last letter in the word. Then write the word.

1. we____ _____

2. chai____ _____

3. bel____ _____

4. coo____ _____

5. tu____ _____

6.  bea____ _____

7. snai____ _____

8. for____ _____

9. gir____ _____

10. bi____ _____

Score: ____/10

Sounds and Letters: *F, G, H, D, W*

A Match the Sounds

Name the first picture. Listen to the first sound and note the letter.
Circle the picture with the same first sound. The first one is done for you.

1.

2.

3.

4.

5.

Score: / 5

B Match the Sounds and Letters

Name the word for each picture. Circle the letter that begins the word.

1.   f   g   h   d   w

2.   f   g   h   d   w

3.   f   g   h   d   w

4.   f   g   h   d   w

5.   f   g   h   d   w

Name the word for each picture. Circle the letter that ends the word.

6.   f   g   h   d   w

7.   f   g   h   d   w

8.   f   g   h   d   w

9.   f   g   h   d   w

10.   f   g   h   d   w

Score: ☐ / 10

C Spell the Sounds

Name the word for each picture. Write the first letter in the word. Then write the word.

1. ___eb _____

2. ___at _____

3. ___un _____

4. ___oor _____

5. ___an _____

6. ___ish _____

7. ___ire _____

8. ___orm _____

9. ___oat _____

10. ___and _____

Score: /10

D Spell the Sounds

Name the word for each picture. Write the last letter in the word. Then write the word.

1. roo___   _____

2. fla___   _____

3. brea___   _____

4. fro___   _____

5. sle___   _____

6. shel___   _____

7. be___   _____

8. wi___   _____

9. lea___   _____

10. pi___   _____

Sounds and Letters: *V, C, Y, Z, Q*

Ⓐ Match the Sounds

Name the first picture. Listen to the first sound and note the letter.
Circle the picture with the same first sound.

1.

2.

3.

4.

5.

Score: ⁄ 5

B Match the Sounds and Letters

Name the word for each picture. Circle the letter that begins the word.

1.   v   c   y   z   q

2.   v   c   y   z   q

3.   v   c   y   z   q

4.   v   c   y   z   q

5.   v   c   y   z   q

6.   v   c   y   z   q

7.   v   c   y   z   q

8.   v   c   y   z   q

9.   v   c   y   z   q

10.   v   c   y   z   q

C Spell the Sounds

Name the word for each picture. Write the first letter in the word. Then write the word.

1. ___an _____

2. ___amel _____

3. ___o-yo _____

4. ___ipper _____

5. ___uarter _____

6. ___ow _____

7. ___arn _____

8. ___est _____

9. ___ueen _____

10. ___ebra _____

Ⓓ Spell the Sounds

Name the word for each picture. Write the first letter in the word on the short line. Then write the new word.

1. e___ual _____

2. sto___e _____

3. law___er _____

4. s___uare _____

5. fa___t _____

6. qui___ _____

7. ___ear _____

8. se___en _____

9. a___t _____

10. la___y _____

Unit 1 Review

Match the Sounds

Name the first picture. Circle the picture with the same first sound.

Sample

1.

2.

3.

4.

5.

6.

7.

8.

GO ON →

Matching Sounds

Name the word for each picture. Write the letter that begins the word.

9. _____

10. _____

11. _____

12. _____

13. _____

14. _____

15. _____

16. _____

17. _____

18. _____

19. _____

20.  _____

21. _____

22. _____

23.  _____

24. _____

25. _____

26. _____

27. _____

28. _____

STOP

Score: ___/28

The Vowel Sound in *Hat* and *Map*

Ⓐ Check the Meaning

Word List			
gas	hat	fast	cash
man	ran	map	flag

Write the missing list word.

1. One day a _____ named Ed went for a ride. He loved his new car.

2. There was not much _____ in the tank. Ed forgot to check.

3. Ed was too happy to care. He just drove very _____ down a lonely road.

4. Then his car stopped. Ed got out of the car. He took off his _____ and rubbed his head.

5. Ed was lost and out of gas. What should he do? He decided to check a _____ .

6. He made a _____ out of a rag. Then he waved it at a bus. The bus stopped for him.

7. Ed _____ to the bus. A smile came to his face.

8. It did not last long. He put a hand in his pocket. He had no _____ to ride the bus or buy gas.

Add two more sentences. Use two list words.

9. _____

_____

10. _____

_____

B Study the Spelling

Change one letter. Write a list word.

1. last _____

2. cap _____

3. mash _____

4. flap _____

Add the missing letter. Write a list word.

5. f___ag _____

6. ca___h _____

7. ___as _____

8. ra___ _____

9. ___at _____

10. ma___ _____

Write the list word or words for each of these clues.

Two words that rhyme with *tan* and *can*.

11. _____

12. _____

Three words that have four letters.

13. _____

15. _____

14. _____

It is the missing word.

16. I see, I saw; I say, I said; I run, I _____

Move the mixed-up letters. Write four list words.

17. staf _____

18. arn _____

19. chas _____

20. nam _____

21. galf _____

22. pam _____

23. sag _____

24. aht _____

ⓒ Build Your Skills

Spelling Tutor

The middle sound you hear in *hat* and *map* is called the short *a* sound. This vowel sound is often spelled with the letter *a*.

h<u>a</u>t   m<u>a</u>p

Add an *a*. Write a list word. Read the word out loud or to yourself.

1. m___p _____

2. h___t _____

3. f___st _____

4. g___s _____

5. r___n _____

6. fl___g _____

Change the vowel to *a*. Write a new word. Read the word out loud or to yourself.

7. bed _____

8. lost _____

9. lip _____

10. pick _____

11. sick _____

12. stump _____

13. buck _____

14. dish _____

15. pin _____

16. cup _____

17. tip _____

18. crush _____

19. then _____

20. fit _____

21. ring _____

22. fin _____

23. ten _____

24. limb _____

25. fun _____

26. pitch _____

27. lend _____

28. clump _____

Score: /28

D Proofread and Write

Joe wrote this list of things to do. He made three spelling mistakes. Draw a
line through each misspelled word. Write the word correctly above it.

Things to Do

1. Make a faste trip to the bank.

2. Cash my check.

3. Put gass in the car.

4. Look for my old hat.

5. Fix the rip in the fleg.

6. Take a map to the man at work.

Writing Folder

Make a list of things you need to do. Write your list on another
sheet of paper. Use at least three list words.

Proofread your list. Correct any mistakes. Make a clean copy and put
it in your writing folder.

The Vowel Sound in *Pen* and *Wet*

Ⓐ Check the Meaning

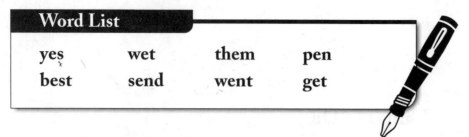

Word List

yes	wet	them	pen
best	send	went	get

Write the missing list word.

1. TV ads make it easy to say _____.

2. Everything looks good on TV. What you _____ may not look so good.

3. Think before you _____ your money in the mail. Know what you are buying.

4. If you buy a _____, be sure it has ink in it.

5. If you buy some pants, ask if a belt comes with _____.

6. The new red hat looked fine. The buyer _____ for a walk in the rain.

7. She learned a lesson. Some colors run when they become _____.

8. There are many ways to shop. The _____ way is to see what you are getting first.

Add two more sentences. Use two list words.

9. _____

_____

10. _____

_____

Score: ___ / 10

ⓑ Study the Spelling

Change one letter. Write a list word.

1. then _____

2. yet _____

3. sand _____

4. bent _____

5. got _____

6. pet _____

7. rest _____

8. web _____

Write a list word or words for each clue.

9. good, better, _____

10. Add a letter to *wet*. _____

11. It begins like *pin* and ends like *ten*. _____

12. They rhyme. _____ _____

13. It begins like *yellow* and rhymes with *mess*. _____

Write the list words with four letters. Circle the consonants.

14. _____

15. _____

16. _____

17. _____

Write the list word that fits each space.

18.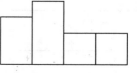

19.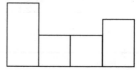

20.

C Build Your Skills

Spelling Tutor

The middle sound you hear in *pen* and *wet* is called the short e sound. This vowel sound is often spelled with the letter *e*.

p<u>e</u>t   w<u>e</u>t

Add an *e*. Write a list word. Read the word out loud or to yourself.

1. b___st _____

2. w___t _____

3. y___s _____

4. p___n _____

5. g___t _____

6. th___m _____

7. w___nt _____

8. s___nd _____

Change the vowel to *e*. Write a new word. Read the word out loud or to yourself.

9. band _____

10. not _____

11. sat _____

12. and _____

13. bill _____

14. bolt _____

15. mat _____

16. tan _____

17. log _____

18. rust _____

19. fill _____

20. disk _____

21. man _____

22. dock _____

23. bit _____

24. pack _____

25. put _____

26. bag _____

27. sit _____

28. bud _____

29. bond _____

30. sand _____

Ⓓ Proofread and Write

Nan wants to put this ad in the paper. She made three spelling mistakes.
Draw a line through each misspelled word. Write the word correctly above it.

Car for Sale

Get a car that is like new. The tires are in

good shape. I have tham checked often.

They never slip on wet roads. Last year I

wendt 400 miles on a tank of gas.

$100 or bast offer.

Call Nan at 555-0987.

Write an ad for something you want to sell. Use at least three list words.

_____

_____

_____

_____

_____

Writing Folder

Proofread your ad. Correct any mistakes. Make a clean copy and put it
in your writing folder.

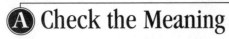

The Vowel Sound in *Big* and *Win*

Ⓐ Check the Meaning

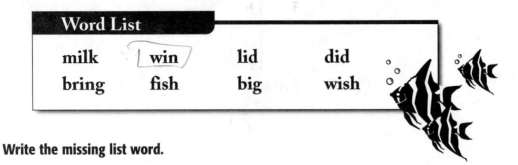

Word List

milk	win	lid	did
bring	fish	big	wish

Write the missing list word.

1. Make your food money buy more. You can _____ this fight.

2. Do not guess what you need. Always _____ a shopping list.

3. A list will be a _____ help. You will get only what you need.

4. Do not buy more _____ than you can drink. It will not stay fresh.

5. You will _____ you had saved your cash.

6. There is no need to buy meat. Eat _____. It is better for you to eat.

7. Do not buy a jar with a bad _____. What is inside may be no good.

8. Shop smart. You will be glad you _____.

Add two more sentences. Use two list words.

9. _____

   _____

10. _____

    _____

B Study the Spelling

Write the list words that fit the boxes.

1. | w | | |

2. (boxes with **l**)

3. | b | | |

4. 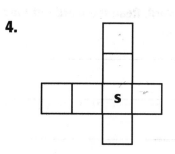 (boxes with **s**)

Circle the words that are the same. Then write them.

5. did bid bib did hid lid _____

6. bag big dig beg lid big _____

7. mild smile milk nick milk _____

8. hid lip dip lid did lid _____

9. ring bring brake bring broke _____

Write the list words with four or more letters. Circle the consonants.

10. _____   12. _____

11. _____   13. _____

Write *did* and *fish*. Write a list word that rhymes with each word.

14. _____   _____

15. _____   _____

Ⓒ Build Your Skills

Spelling Tutor

**The middle sound you hear in *big* and *win* is called the short i
sound. This vowel sound is often spelled with the letter *i*.**

b<u>i</u>g   w<u>i</u>n

Add an *i*. Write a list word. Read the word out loud or to yourself.

1. w___sh _____

2. b___g _____

3. f__sh _____

4. w___n _____

5. d___d _____

6. l___d _____

7. m___lk _____

8. br___ng _____

Add an *i*. Write a new word. Read the word out loud or to yourself.

9. h___d _____

10. s___t _____

11. d___g _____

12. th___n _____

13. bl___nk _____

14. d___m _____

15. p___g _____

16. h___m _____

17. th___s _____

18. k___ss _____

19. cl___p _____

20. dr___nk _____

21. fl___p _____

22. pr___nt _____

23. c___ty _____

24. br___ck _____

25. qu___z _____

26. h___ll _____

27. s___nk _____

28. k___ck _____

29. l___mp _____

30. l___p _____

Score: ⟋ 30

D Proofread and Write

Read this shopping list. Find four spelling mistakes. Draw a line through each misspelled word. Write the word correctly above it.

Shopping List

2 big fich①

②
Breng back old bags.

1 jar of jam. Check the lid.

③
Skim millk

④
Fill out form to wen a cash prize.

Make your own shopping list. Use at least three list words.

_____

_____

_____

_____

_____

_____

Writing Folder

Proofread your list. Correct any mistakes. Make a clean copy and put it in your writing folder.

The Vowel Sound in *Job* and *Box*

Ⓐ Check the Meaning

Word List

box	flop	shock	spot
knock	got	job	stop

Write the missing list word.

1. It was time to quit. Workers were closing the lid on the tool _____.

2. One was cleaning up an oil _____ on the floor.

3. Then there was a _____ on the door. The owner of the mill came into the room.

4. She said the mill was closing. They would _____ making steel parts.

5. This was a _____ to the workers. Each worker had to make a plan.

6. Their pay would end in six weeks. Everyone would need to find a new _____.

7. All were very sad. Some wanted to _____ into a chair and just sit.

8. Others had a better idea. They _____ a copy of a paper. They saw the Help Wanted ads.

Add two more sentences. Use two list words.

9. _____

_____

10. _____

_____

Score: / 10

B Study the Spelling

One word in each group is spelled wrong. Circle the misspelled word. Write it correctly.

1. shock   folp   got   _____

2. stop   box   jop   _____

3. knok   spot   stop   _____

4. shok   job   flop   _____

Write the list word or words for each of these clues.

5. It begins and ends with the same letter. _____

6. It rhymes with *fox*. _____

7. Mix the letters in *spot* to make this word. _____

8. Change one letter in *sob* to make this word. _____

9. It begins like *get* and ends like *hot*. _____

10. It begins like *she* and ends like *dock*. _____

11. They are two words that rhyme with *pop*. _____
_____

12. They are the list words with five letters.

_____ _____

Add the missing letters. Write a list word.

13. f___ ___p _____

14. s___oc___ _____

15. bo___ _____

16. s___ot _____

17. s___op _____

18. ___ob _____

19. ___noc___ _____

20. go___ _____

Score: ◻/20

C Build Your Skills

Spelling Tutor

The middle sound you hear in *job* and *box* is called the short o sound. This vowel sound is often spelled with the letter *o*.

j o b   b o x

Add an *o*. Write a list word. Read the word out loud or to yourself.

1. b___x _____

2. st___p _____

3. fl___p _____

4. j___b _____

5. sh___ck _____

6. kn___ck _____

7. sp___t _____

8. g___t _____

Add an *o*. Write a list word. Read the word out loud or to yourself.

9. ___dd _____

10. ch___p _____

11. b___dy _____

12. c___py _____

13. j___g _____

14. kn___t _____

15. f___x _____

16. bl___ck _____

17. b___mb _____

18. h___t _____

19. sh___p _____

20. r___bin _____

21. c___met _____

22. m___p _____

23. r___ck _____

24. p___cket _____

25. p___nd _____

26. h___ckey _____

27. l___ck _____

28. fl___ck _____

Score: /28

D Proofread and Write

Read the Help Wanted ad below. Find three spelling mistakes. Draw a line through each misspelled word. Write the word correctly above it.

HELP WANTED

Stop looking! We have gat the jab for you!

Pack pens in a box. Send them to the right spot.

Good pay. Knok on our door or send these facts

to The Ace Company, Box 125, Hazlet, NJ 07730:

Your name   The pay you want

Your address   What makes you a
                             good worker
Your last job
                             Something about
                             yourself

Write the facts asked for in the ad. Use at least three list words.

_____

_____

_____

_____

_____

Writing Folder

Proofread your answer to the ad. Correct any mistakes. Make a clean copy and put it in your writing folder.

Unit 2 Review

Finish the Meaning

Find the missing word. Fill in the circle next to it.

Sample

Put ice in the water.
I want a _____ drink.
- ● cold
- ○ new
- ○ funny

1. Do not drop the ink.
   It will make a _____ on the rug.
   - ○ map
   - ○ pen
   - ○ spot

2. The dog began to bark.
   It heard a _____ on the door.
   - ○ lid
   - ○ knock
   - ○ wish

3. It will be cold.
   You must _____ a coat.
   - ○ win
   - ○ flop
   - ○ bring

4. June got 100 percent on her test.
   She is the _____ speller in the class.
   - ○ best
   - ○ big
   - ○ win

5. Hank was tired.
   He decided to _____ into a soft chair.
   - ○ stop
   - ○ flop
   - ○ wish

6. Fred wanted to get extra money.
   He took a second _____.
   - ○ job
   - ○ man
   - ○ map

7. We had never been there before.
   We got a _____ to keep from getting lost.
   - ○ pen
   - ○ map
   - ○ lid

8. Her death was a surprise.
   It was a _____ to all of us.
   - ○ shock
   - ○ fish
   - ○ stop

GO ON ➤

Check the Spelling

Fill in the circle next to the word that is spelled correctly and best completes the sentence.

9. Pick up the papers and put _____ in the box.

○ them ○ thum
○ tham ○ tem

10. Please _____ the bus. I want to get off.

○ stoap ○ stup
○ stap ○ stop

11. We _____ to the beach last night.

○ want ○ wendt
○ went ○ wunt

12. I lost my credit card so I paid with _____.

○ cash ○ cashe
○ cach ○ chash

13. I try to _____ a letter to her each week.

○ sand ○ scend
○ send ○ cend

14. The band played as the _____ was raised.

○ fleg ○ flaeg
○ flage ○ flag

15. The mower would not start without _____ in its tank.

○ guas ○ gaes
○ gas ○ gaz

16. You must be a very _____ skater to play this game.

○ fast ○ flast
○ fest ○ faest

17. We answered _____ to every question.

○ yest ○ yes
○ yas ○ yess

18. After the rain, everything was _____.

○ wat ○ whet
○ wet ○ wut

Score: ◻/18

STOP

Review 45

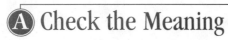

The Vowel Sound in *Jump* and *Lunch*

Ⓐ Check the Meaning

Word List			
cup	jump	lunch	must
funny	just	stuck	run

Write the missing list word.

1. Kim is in a hurry. She _____ be at work by one o'clock.

2. She has no time to eat _____. Kim will eat on the way.

3. First she has to _____ into her car and start for work.

4. There is a shop on the way. She can get a _____ of hot soup.

5. It is almost one o'clock. Kim has _____ ten more minutes.

6. Now she is _____ on the road. No cars are moving.

7. Some may want to laugh. But Kim does not feel this is _____.

8. Maybe it would be faster to _____ to work.

Add two more sentences. Use a list word in each sentence.

9. _____

_____

10. _____

_____

Score: /10

B Study the Spelling

Write a list word for each clue.

1. It rhymes with *bunch*. _____

2. Change the first letter in *bump* to make this word. _____

3. It begins like *cat* and ends like *pup*. _____

4. It has five letters. The third letter is a vowel. _____

5. Yesterday I ran. Tomorrow I will _____.

6. It has two letters that are same. _____

Write the two list words that rhyme.

7. _____   _____

One word is spelled wrong in each group. Circle the word. Then write it correctly.

8. cup   funy   just   jump   _____

9. run   stuk   must   lunch   _____

10. jump   just   lanch   cup   _____

11. funny   runn   must   stuck   _____

Unscramble the letters. Write the list words.

12. mupj _____   14. sjut _____

13. stum _____   15. upc _____

© Build Your Skills

Spelling Tutor

The middle sound in *cup* and *run* is called the short u sound.
The short u sound is often spelled with the letter *u*.

c<u>u</u>p   r<u>u</u>n

Add *u*. Write a list word.

1. st__ck _____

2. r__n _____

3. l__nch _____

4. j__st _____

5. f__nny _____

6. c__p _____

7. j__mp _____

8. m__st _____

Add *u*. Write a new word.

9. dr__m _____

10. tr__ck _____

11. s__ch _____

12. s__n _____

13. __nder _____

14. s__mmer _____

15. S__nday _____

16. cl__b _____

17. b__s _____

18. __p _____

19. m__d _____

20. __gly _____

Score: ___ / 20

D Proofread and Write

Read these shop signs. Find three spelling mistakes. Cross out each misspelled word. Then write the word correctly above it.

Large cup of tea
50 cents

Lanch Sale!
Ham Sandwich . . . $1.95
You must try one!

**Everyone mast
wear shoes!**

Fresh Pies
They jast came out
of the oven!

Take some food home.
Don't run out!

Our cakes may look funny,
but they are good to eat.

Writing Folder

On another sheet of paper, write four signs for a store. Use at least one list word in each sign.

Then proofread your signs. Correct any mistakes. Make a clean copy and put it in your writing folder.

The Vowel Sounds in *We* and *Go*

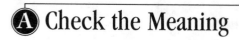

(A) Check the Meaning

Word List			
he	so	open	even
only	go	she	we

Write the missing list word.

1. Meg and Dave need to buy food. They have no eggs or milk. They are _____ out of bread.

2. Meg's dad is coming for lunch. They must _____ to the store.

3. Dave looks for food ads in the paper. _____ finds a store having a big sale.

4. The ad says in big letters: "_____ sell food for less!"

5. The store is _____ until six o'clock. There is no need to hurry.

6. Meg checks the price tags. _____ is glad to see such low prices.

7. Apples are _____ ten cents each.

8. It pays to find a sale. Watch the food ads _____ that you can save money too.

Add two more sentences. Use a list word in each sentence.

9. _____

_____

10. _____

_____

Score: ___ / 10

B Study the Spelling

Words have parts called *syllables.* You hear the parts when you say a word.
The word *sad* has one syllable. The word *baby* has two syllables, *ba-by*.

Read the list words and listen to the syllables. Write the list words with
two syllables.

1. _____   3. _____

2. _____

Find four list words. Circle the words. Then write them on the lines. One is
done for you.

d	o	p	w	e	g
x	p	s	o	b	y
c	e	h	s	h	o
v	n	e	f	h	w
d	m	e	s	e	k

4. __we_____

5. _____

6. _____

7. _____

Write the list words that fit each clue.

Two list words that rhyme with *no.*

8. _____   9. _____

Three list words that rhyme with *me.*

10. _____   12. _____

11. _____

Write *open, she,* and *only.* Circle the word you see within each word.

13. _____   15. _____

14. _____

© Build Your Skills

Spelling Tutor

The last sound in *he* and *she* is called the long e sound. The long e sound is sometimes spelled with the letter *e*.

h<u>e</u>   sh<u>e</u>

The last sound in *go* and *so* is called the long o sound. The long o sound is sometimes spelled with the letter *o*.

g<u>o</u>   s<u>o</u>

Write the list words. Circle the letter that spells the long e or the long o sound.

1. _____

2. _____

3. _____

4. _____

5. _____

6. _____

7. _____

8. _____

Add _e_ or _o_. Write a new word.

9. b___   _____

10. s___fa   _____

11. p___ny   _____

12. b___low   _____

13. ___qual   _____

14. b___nus   _____

15. s___da   _____

16. b___ing   _____

17. b___tween   _____

18. f___ld   _____

19. t___tal   _____

20. f___ver   _____

21. ___vil   _____

22. c___zy   _____

23. h___ly   _____

24. m___tor   _____

25. r___al   _____

26. v___to   _____

Score: / 26

D Proofread and Write

Here is a note Meg wrote. She made four spelling mistakes. Cross out each
misspelled word. Spell the word correctly above it.

Things to keep in mind:

1. We have onely one egg. Go to the store and get more eggs.

2. The store is not opan on Sunday. Don't go then.

3. Call Dave so hee will stop to get bread.

4. Joe's store has good prices. The sale makes them evan better.

Write a note to yourself. List some things you want to do. Use at least three
list words.

_____

_____

_____

_____

_____

_____

Writing Folder

Proofread your work. Correct any mistakes. Make a clean copy and put it
in your writing folder.

The Vowel Sounds in *Kind* and *Old*

Ⓐ Check the Meaning

Word List

most	cold	child	blind
hold	find	kind	sold

Write the missing list word.

1. Children must dress warmly on _____ days. If they do not, they may become ill.

2. A sick _____ needs care. Do you know what to do?

3. Rest is good, but _____ children do not like to stay in bed.

4. Your children may be like that. You need to _____ a way to keep them calm.

5. Try giving them a new toy. It should be one they can _____ in their hands.

6. It does not have to cost much. Toys like this are easy to find. They are _____ in all stores.

7. A story will keep your children calm. Stories are the _____ of thing all children love.

8. A song may also help. Sing the song about the three _____ mice. This may help your children go to sleep.

Add two more sentences. Use a list word in each sentence.

9. _____

_____

10. _____

_____

Score: / 10

B Study the Spelling

Write *sold*. Write two list words that rhyme with *sold*.

1. _____   3. _____

2. _____

Write *find*. Write two list words that rhyme with *find*.

4. _____   6. _____

5. _____

Add the missing letters. Write the list word.

7. ___ost _____   12. ___lin___ _____

8. hol___ _____   13. ___hil___ _____

9. b___ ___nd _____   14. f___ ___d _____

10. c___i___d _____   15. s___ ___d _____

11. ki___d _____

Write the list word or words for each clue.

16. They begin with two consonants.

_____ _____

17. It can be found in the word *soldier*. _____

18. It begins with the same sound as the word *cat*. The first letter is a *k*.

_____

Write the list words that fit each space.

19. 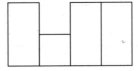   20.

C Build Your Skills

Spelling Tutor

The vowel sound in *find* and *child* is called the long i sound. The long i sound is sometimes spelled with the letter *i*.

$$\text{f\underline{i}nd} \qquad \text{ch\underline{i}ld}$$

The vowel sound in *most* and *cold* is called the long o sound. The long o sound is sometimes spelled with the letter *o*.

$$\text{m\underline{o}st} \qquad \text{c\underline{o}ld}$$

Write the list words. Circle the letter that spells the long vowel sound.

1. _____

2. _____

3. _____

4. _____

5. _____

6. _____

7. _____

8. _____

Add *i* or *o*. Write a new word.

9. t___ld _____

10. p___nt _____

11. sc___ld _____

12. gh___st _____

13. beh___nd _____

14. gr___nd _____

15. b___ld _____

16. s___gn _____

17. b___th _____

18. b___lt _____

19. w___nd _____

20. c___lt _____

21. p___st _____

22. cl___mb _____

23. g___ld _____

24. w___ld _____

Score: / 24

Ⓓ Proofread and Write

This note was left for a babysitter. Three words were misspelled. Cross out each misspelled word. Write the word correctly above it.

To the babysitter:

• You will fiend a cold soda on

    the table.

• Hold my childe if she cries.

• Read her the story about the three

    blind mice.

• It is most kidn of you to help me.

Write a note to someone. Use at least three list words.

_____

_____

_____

_____

Writing Folder

Proofread your work. Correct any mistakes. Make a clean copy and put it in your writing folder.

Key Words

Ⓐ Check the Meaning

Word List			
very	were	said	come
are	does	any	you

Write the missing list word.

1. I must take a test. It is a _____ big test. It will let me stay in the United States.

2. I think it is the same test _____ took last year.

3. I tried to get ready. I did not have _____ books.

4. I went to a bookstore. I saw many books, but they _____ all over $5.00.

5. A bookstore _____ not let people use books. People must buy books.

6. I asked Mike what to do. He _____ I can get books at the library.

7. He asked me to _____ with him. We got all the books I needed. They were free.

8. Now I think I will pass the test. We _____ in a great country!

Add two more sentences. Use two list words.

9. _____

_____

10. _____

_____

Score: /10

B Study the Spelling

Add the missing letter or letters. Write a list word.

1. a___e _____

2. c___me _____

3. y___ ___ _____

4. w___r___ _____

5. ___e___y _____

6. d___e___ _____

Write the word or words for each clue.

7. It rhymes with *some*. _____

8. It rhymes with *car*. _____

9. Two words that end with *y*.

_____ _____

10. Today I say it. Last night I _____ it.

11. Two words that have two syllables.

_____ _____

12. Not me or him. _____

Write the list word that fits each shape. Cover the words with a piece of paper. Picture each word with your eyes closed. Now write each word on another piece of paper.

13.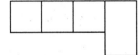

14.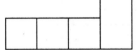

15.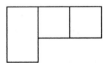

16.

17.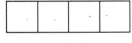

18.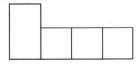

C Build Your Skills

Spelling Tutor

Words are placed in a dictionary in alphabetical or ABC order. The order of the alphabet is shown below.

a b c d e f g h i j k l m n o p q u r s t u v w x y z

Words that begin with *a* come before words that begin with *b*. Sometimes words have the same first letter. When this happens, use the second letter to put the words in alphabetical order. The groups of words below are in alphabetical order.

does	come	any
said	were	are
very	you	come

Fill in the missing letter of the alphabet.

1. a___c

2. f___h

3. j___l

4. x___z

5. m___o

6. d___f

7. u___w

8. b___d

9. o___q

10. h___j

11. r___t

12. k___m

Write the words in alphabetical order.

13. box   man   fish

_____

_____

_____

14. job   boy   hop

_____

_____

_____

15. cute   star   home

_____

_____

_____

16. pig   big   yes

_____

_____

_____

Score: ___ 16

⒟ Proofread and Write

Kim sent this letter to the library. She made three spelling mistakes. Cross out each misspelled word. Spell the word correctly above it.

112 Farm Road
Reading, PA 19605
May 18, 1997

Reading Library
698 Main Street
Reading, PA 19605

Dear Madam or Sir:

Your books are a vary big help. Thank you for letting me use them for my test. I would like to get my own card. This way I can take out eny books I need.

You sayed I should ask for a form. I will fill it out and send it back to you. Maybe I can come by and give it to you.

Thanks again,

Kim Smith

Kim Smith

Writing Folder

Write a letter to your library. Use your own paper. Ask how you can get a card. Use at least three list words.

Proofread your letter. Correct any mistakes. Then mail your letter or put it in your writing folder.

Unit 3 Review

Complete the Meaning

Fill in the circle next to the word that best completes each sentence.

1. Sid makes us laugh. His jokes are very _____.
   - ○ blind
   - ○ funny
   - ○ open

2. Fred had two cars. He _____ one of them.
   - ○ sold
   - ○ said
   - ○ went

3. Beth cannot go out alone. She is just a _____.
   - ○ cup
   - ○ child
   - ○ lunch

4. Ben went to town. _____ will look for a job there.
   - ○ We
   - ○ He
   - ○ She

5. Speak up. We want to hear what is _____.
   - ○ said
   - ○ open
   - ○ ran

6. No one can get in after one o'clock. You _____ be there on time.
   - ○ open
   - ○ were
   - ○ must

7. I do not want to eat now. I just had a big _____.
   - ○ lunch
   - ○ cup
   - ○ jump

8. My arms were full. Jane had to _____ the door for me.
   - ○ find
   - ○ hold
   - ○ jump

9. The dog was lost in the woods. It took all day to _____ her.
   - ○ find
   - ○ go
   - ○ run

10. I have four cats. I do not want _____ more.
    - ○ only
    - ○ any
    - ○ very

GO ON ▶

Check the Spelling

Choose the word that is spelled correctly and best completes the sentence.

11. I don't have a car, but Ellen

    _____.
    - ○ duz
    - ○ doz
    - ○ does

12. I tried to open the door, but it was _____.
    - ○ stuck
    - ○ stuk
    - ○ stek

13. Alicia has three cats and two dogs. She _____ has a bird.
    - ○ eeven
    - ○ even
    - ○ evin

14. If he turns off the lights, we will be _____.
    - ○ blynd
    - ○ bliand ←
    - ○ blind

15. _____ people like Jerome. He is a nice person.
    - ○ Most
    - ○ Moast
    - ○ Moest

16. Put on a jacket when it is

    _____.
    - ○ kold
    - ○ cold
    - ○ colde

17. What _____ of sandwich did she order?
    - ○ kind
    - ○ kynd
    - ○ cind

18. They don't want to talk to him. They want to talk to _____.
    - ○ yu
    - ○ yew
    - ○ you

19. When _____ they coming home?
    - ○ are
    - ○ ar
    - ○ ahr

20. She will _____ to class tomorrow.
    - ○ com
    - ○ come
    - ○ cume

STOP

13 Vowel-Consonant-*e* Words

Ⓐ Check the Meaning

> **Word List**
>
> | these | nose | ride | use |
> |-------|------|------|------|
> | make | wide | lake | plate |

Write the missing list word.

1. Trips can be fun. Always _____ a list of things to take. This will make the trip easier.

2. A boat on a _____ can be fun. The hot sun might burn your skin.

3. Take a cream to block the sun. Put a lot on your _____ and around your eyes. This cream should be on your list.

4. What if there is no picnic table? You may have to sit on the ground. Take a blanket. It should be long and _____.

5. It is easier if you eat from a paper _____. It cannot break, and it does not need to be washed.

6. You can also _____ plastic forks and spoons.

7. Take a soft pad in the car. Children can sleep as they _____.

8. There are many things to put on your list. _____ are just a few of them.

Add two more sentences. Use a list word in each sentence.

9. _____

   _____

10. _____

   _____

Score: / 10

Ⓑ Study the Spelling

Write the list word or words for each of these clues.

1. These two words rhyme with .

    _____ _____

2. It begins like ⟋ . _____

3. They begin with two consonants. _____

    _____

4. These two words have the same vowel sound you hear in *ice*.

    _____ _____

5. It begins like *went* and ends like *side*. _____

6. It has three letters. Two of them are vowels. _____

Add the missing letters. Write a list word.

7. no___e _____

8. p___at___ _____

9. l___k___ _____

10. r___ ___e _____

11. w___d___ _____

12. ___s___ _____

Write *wide, use,* and *these* in alphabetical order.

13. _____

14. _____

15. _____

C Build Your Skills

Spelling Tutor

The words *lake*, *these*, *wide*, *nose*, and *use* have long vowel sounds.
Long vowel sounds are sometimes spelled vowel–consonant–*e*.

long a sound	l<u>ake</u>
long e sound	th<u>ese</u>
long i sound	w<u>ide</u>
long o sound	n<u>ose</u>
long u sound	<u>use</u>

Write the list words. Circle the vowel-consonant-*e* spelling.

1. _____   5. _____

2. _____   6. _____

3. _____   7. _____

4. _____   8. _____

Add the missing letters. Write two new words with the long a sound.

9. g___v___ _____   11. pl___t___ _____

10. s___v___ _____   12. n___m___ _____

Add the missing letters. Write two new words with the long i sound.

13. f___v___ _____   15. cr___m___ _____

14. s___z___ _____   16. s___d___ _____

Add the missing letters. Write two new words with the long o sound.

17. b___n___ _____   19. th___s___ _____

18. h___p___ _____   20. st___n___ _____

Score: / 20

D Proofread and Write

Here is a list of things to do. The list has three spelling mistakes. Draw a line through each misspelled word. Then write the word correctly above it.

These things must get done today!

- Put out a plaet of food for the dog.

- Make the beds. Uze clean sheets.

- Try to find a ride to the lake.

- Check the hall. See how wyde it is. Then buy a rug.

- Take something to keep my nose from running.

Make a list of things you must do this week. Use at least three list words.

_____

_____

_____

_____

_____

_____

 Writing Folder

Proofread your list. Correct any mistakes. Make a clean copy and put it in your writing folder.

More Long Vowel Words

Ⓐ Check the Meaning

Word List

| show | float | rain | sleep |
| play | eat | boat | trail |

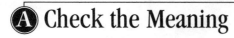

Write the missing list word.

1. To stay fit, you must _____ right.

2. Get a chart of the foods you should eat. It will _____ you good things to eat, like bread and cereal.

3. There are other things you can do. One thing is to get seven hours of _____ every night.

4. Next you need to work your body. Boys and girls do this when they _____ outside.

5. The sun does not have to be shining. Children will run and jump even in the _____.

6. Men and women are not as active. They may just _____ in a swimming pool. This is not much work.

7. Some may sit in a _____ on a lake and fish.

8. It is better to take a long hike on a rocky _____. This is not easy, but it is good for you.

Add two more sentences. Use at least one list word in each sentence.

9. _____

_____

10. _____

_____

B Study the Spelling

Change one letter. Write a list word.

1. raid _____
2. clay _____
3. coat _____

4. train _____
5. snow _____
6. steep _____

Write the list word that fits each clue.

7. It begins with two vowels. _____

8. It ends with the long a sound. _____

9. It ends with the long o sound. _____

10. It begins like *trip* and ends like *nail*. _____

11. It begins like *slap* and ends like *creep*. _____

Write the four list words with four letters. Circle the vowels.

12. _____
13. _____

14. _____
15. _____

One word in each group is misspelled. Circle the misspelled word. Write it correctly.

16. eat   bote   rain   _____
17. tral   show   play   _____
18. float   boat   eet   _____

Write the list word that fits each shape.

19.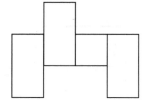

20.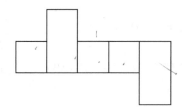

C Build Your Skills

Spelling Tutor

Some long vowels are spelled with two letters.

long a	r<u>ai</u>n	pl<u>ay</u>
long e	sl<u>ee</u>p	<u>ea</u>t
long o	b<u>oa</u>t	sh<u>ow</u>

Write the list words. Circle the letters that spell the long vowel sound.

1. _____

2. _____

3. _____

4. _____

5. _____

6. _____

7. _____

8. _____

Add the missing letters. Write a new long vowel word.

9. Are you afr____ ____d of the dark? (long a) _____

10. Take the subwa____ to town. (long a) _____

11. She will thr____ ____ the ball. (long o) _____

12. We drove down the r____ad. (long o) _____

13. Do you add cr____am to your coffee? (long e) _____

14. We got four inches of sn____w this winter. (long o) _____

15. I will k____ ____p the present. (long e) _____

16. I eat cereal from a large b____wl. (long o) _____

17. The rain will del____ ____ the game. (long a) _____

18. Our team has a new c____ach. (long o) _____

Score: ____ / 18

Ⓓ Proofread and Write

This ad for a summer fitness camp has three spelling mistakes. Draw a line through each misspelled word. Write the word correctly above it.

Camp Goodbody

At our camp, you . . .

- eat only good food

- get lots of sleap

- row a bote to class

- walk an old wagon trale

- play games like baseball and soccer

In case of rain, we have a tent.

Write an ad for something that is good for you. Use at least three list words.

_____

_____

_____

_____

_____

_____

Writing Folder

Proofread your ad. Correct any mistakes. Make a clean copy and put it in your writing folder.

15 The Final Sound in *Kick* and *Dock*

Ⓐ Check the Meaning

Word List

black	dock	kick	pick
rock	sick	snack	stick

Write the missing list word.

1. Nothing beats a day at the park. We will try to _____ a table in the shade.

2. This park has a lake. Boats are tied to a _____ in the lake.

3. Did you bring a football? Try to _____ it over the goal.

4. Be careful! Do not trip and fall on that _____.

5. The children cannot wait for dinner. They can eat a _____ now.

6. Later we will toast marshmallows. We will hold them over the fire on a branch or a _____.

7. Try not to hold the marshmallows too close to the fire. They may burn and become _____.

8. Do not let the children eat too many sweets. They may become _____.

Add two more sentences. Use at least one list word in each sentence.

9. _____

_____

10. _____

_____

B Study the Spelling

Write the list word that fits the sentence. It will rhyme with the underlined word.

1. She carried a _____ in a paper <u>sack</u>.

2. He broke the <u>lock</u> with a big, heavy _____.

3. A fast choice is a <u>quick</u> _____.

4. Big waves on the lake will <u>rock</u> the _____.

5. Ed's dog can do a <u>trick</u>. It can pick up a _____.

Write the list words that begin with two consonants. Circle the beginning consonants.

6. _____

7. _____

8. _____

Add the missing letters. Then write the list word.

9. ki___k _____

10. s___c___ _____

11. b___ac___ _____

12. ___ ___ick _____

13. s___ ___ck _____

14. ro___k _____

15. p___ ___k _____

Write list words for these clues.

16. They have the vowel sound you hear in *hot* and *job*.

    _____ _____

17. It begins and ends with the same letter. _____

18. Add one letter to *sick* to make this word. _____

19. Take one letter from *crock* to make this word. _____

20. It comes last in alphabetical order. _____

C Build Your Skills

Spelling Tutor

The final consonant sound you hear in *kick* and *dock* is often spelled *ck.*

kic<u>k</u>   doc<u>k</u>   stic<u>k</u>   blac<u>k</u>

Write the list words. Circle the letters that spell the final consonant sound.

1. _____

2. _____

3. _____

4. _____

5. _____

6. _____

7. _____

8. _____

Add the missing letters. Write a new word.

9. The key will open the lo____ ____. _____

10. The clo____ ____ will strike on the hour. _____

11. The baker cut a thi____ ____ slice of bread. _____

12. She used cards to do a magic tri____ ____. _____

13. He wore a chain around his ne____ ____. _____

14. The house was made of red bri____ ____. _____

15. Put a che____ ____ after each correct answer. _____

16. Load the wood on the back of the tru____ ____. _____

17. There was not a spe____ ____ of dust in the house. _____

18. Mark took the wre____ ____ to the junk yard. _____

Score: ⟋ 18

Ⓓ Proofread and Write

This list of park rules has three spelling mistakes. Draw a line through each misspelled word. Write the word correctly above it.

• **PARK RULES** •

Do not run on the boat dock.

Keep off the new black paint.

Do not pik the flowers.

Do not feed scnacks to the ducks.

Keep off the large rock.

Do not break stiks from the trees.

Write a list of rules for your home or yard. Use at least three list words.

_____

_____

_____

_____

_____

_____

Writing Folder

Proofread your list. Correct any mistakes. Make a clean copy and put it in your writing folder.

16 More Key Words

A Check the Meaning

Word List			
every	friend	have	love
many	of	they	was

Write the missing list word.

Dear Susan,

1. Thanks for coming to my baby shower. It _____ good of you to make the trip.

2. I just _____ your gift! The big backpack will come in handy.

3. It is something I really needed. I will use it _____ time I go out.

4. There were so _____ people at the party. It was nice seeing them again.

5. I think I _____ everything I need for the baby.

6. Trina and Gloria kept the party a secret, so _____ must have worked very hard!

7. The notes and cards were the best part _____ all.

8. Your _____ ,

   Elena

Add two more sentences to the letter. Use at least one list word in each sentence.

9. _____

   _____

10. _____

   _____

Score: ⁄ 10

B Study the Spelling

Write a list word for each of these clues.

1. It has just two letters. _____

2. It rhymes with *fuzz.* _____

3. It has six letters. _____

4. It has the word *any* in its spelling. _____

5. It ends with a long a sound spelled *ey.* _____

6. Change one letter in *dove* to make this word. _____

7. It has the word *ever* in its spelling. _____

8. It begins like *ham* and ends like *gave.* _____

Add the missing letters. Write a list word.

9. m___ny _____

10. l___ve _____

11. w___s _____

12. h___ve _____

13. th___y _____

14. m___ny _____

Write the list words that fit the puzzle.

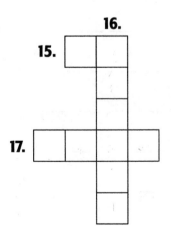

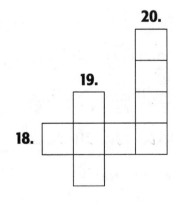

C Build Your Skills

Spelling Tutor

A contraction is made by shortening two words. In a contraction, an apostrophe takes the place of one or more letters.

they are . . . . . they're	he is . . . . he's
you will . . . . . . you'll	is not . . . . isn't
do not . . . . don't	we have . . . . . . we've

Write the two words that were used to make the contractions in these sentences.

1. We've seen that film. _____ _____

2. They're going to go soon. _____ _____

3. We don't own a cat. _____ _____

4. She hasn't seen the book. _____ _____

5. You'll need a coat today. _____ _____

6. This isn't the way home. _____ _____

Copy each sentence. Use a contraction for the underlined words. The first one is done for you.

7. That <u>is not</u> my hat. _That isn't my hat._ _____

8. <u>Do not</u> let me sleep too long. _____

9. I hope <u>you will</u> come on time. _____

10. <u>We have</u> been here before. _____

11. It <u>has not</u> rained today. _____

12. <u>They are</u> working outside. _____

Score: /12

⒟ Proofread and Write

Here is a letter to a store. It has four spelling mistakes. Draw a line through each misspelled word. Write the word correctly above it.

Ed's Budget Barn
606 Brown Road
Marlboro, MA 01752
July 17, 1997

Dear Budget Barn:

I buy meny things at your store. I love most of the things I get from you. The clock I got last week, however, wuz broken. Evry day it stops a few times. The time is never right. I hav sent it back to be fixed three times. It still doesn't work. I would like to get my money back. I will come in on Tuesday with the clock.

Sincerely,

Ned Cook

Ned Cook

Writing Folder

Write a letter to a company. Use your own paper. Tell why you liked or disliked something you bought from the company. Use at least three list words. Proofread your letter, and then make a clean copy. You can mail your letter or keep it in your writing folder.

Unit 4 Review

Finish the Meaning

Find the missing word. Fill in the circle next to the answer.

1. Jill is very tired.
   She will _____ a long time.
   - ○ play
   - ○ eat
   - ○ sleep

2. Kip is going to see a doctor.
   He is _____.
   - ○ sick
   - ○ funny
   - ○ kind

3. Sally is a very good cook. I always
   eat everything on my _____
   when I am at her house.
   - ○ box
   - ○ plate
   - ○ flag

4. Gary needs a ride to work.
   He will ask a _____ to
   take him.
   - ○ child
   - ○ nose
   - ○ friend

5. Paul cannot wait for dinner.
   He will go to the kitchen to
   get a _____.
   - ○ stick
   - ○ snack
   - ○ wish

6. The bed will not fit up the stairs.
   It is too _____.
   - ○ wide
   - ○ cold
   - ○ open

7. There is no place to sit.
   _____ chair is taken.
   - ○ Every
   - ○ Very
   - ○ Any

8. When we get to shore, I will tie
   the boat to the _____.
   - ○ rain
   - ○ show
   - ○ dock

9. A leaf fell in the pool.
   I watched it _____ away.
   - ○ love
   - ○ float
   - ○ hold

10. Fran and Joe are going to the farm.
    _____ will be there for
    two weeks.
    - ○ They
    - ○ He
    - ○ She

GO ON ➡

Check the Spelling

Choose the word that is spelled correctly and best completes the sentence.

11. This winter we had fourteen inches _____ snow.
- ○ uv
- ○ of
- ○ uf
- ○ off

12. Susan likes to go to the movies. She went _____ times last year.
- ○ meny
- ○ mani
- ○ many
- ○ manny

13. He _____ never late for work.
- ○ wuz
- ○ woz
- ○ wus
- ○ was

14. Do you _____ everything you need to fix the pipe?
- ○ have
- ○ haf
- ○ hav
- ○ heve

15. The old coal stove turned _____ from years of use.
- ○ bleck
- ○ black
- ○ blak
- ○ blake

16. Stay on the _____, or you will get lost.
- ○ trail
- ○ trayle
- ○ trale
- ○ tral

17. Use lots of sun cream on your _____ when you go to the beach.
- ○ noze
- ○ nos
- ○ nose
- ○ noz

18. We can see the river from the top of the _____.
- ○ hil
- ○ hile
- ○ hill
- ○ hull

19. Those books are used, but _____ are new.
- ○ tese
- ○ theese
- ○ theze
- ○ these

20. The apples are ripe. We will _____ some and make a pie.
- ○ pik
- ○ pick
- ○ peck
- ○ pike

STOP

17 One Sound, Two Letters

A Check the Meaning

Word List			
class	shall	hill	dress
silly	happy	full	stuff

Write the missing list word.

1. Last week I went to a _____ on job safety.

2. I thought this was a _____ idea. I never get hurt at work. I learned I was wrong.

3. The way you _____ can be unsafe. Some clothes can get caught in motors.

4. Always be very careful with gas. Don't fill a tank too _____. The gas may spill out.

5. Pick up old rags and other _____. You might trip on such things.

6. Some people let dirty rags pile up into a big _____. Don't do this. You can start a fire.

7. Find the nearest doors. If there is a fire, you will be _____ you did.

8. I _____ study the safety rules often.

Add two more sentences. Use at least one list word in each sentence.

9. _____

   _____

10. _____

   _____

Score: / 10

B Study the Spelling

Write the list word or words for each of these clues.

1. Two words with the short u sound you hear in *jump* and *lunch*.

   _____ _____

2. Two words that end with *y*. _____ _____

3. Two words that begin like *ham*. _____ _____

4. A word that begins like *drop* and ends like *less*. _____

5. Two words with just four letters. _____

   _____

6. A word that begins like *clip* and ends like *pass*. _____

7. A word that begins like *ship*. _____

Write the words with five letters. Circle the words with two syllables.

8. _____   11. _____

9. _____   12. _____

10. _____   13. _____

Change one letter. Write a list word.

14. shell _____   17. press _____

15. stiff _____   18. fill _____

16. glass _____

Write the words that fit these shapes.

19. 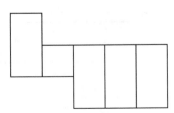   20.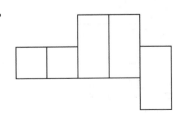

© Build Your Skills

Spelling Tutor

A consonant sound is sometimes spelled with the same two consonant letters.

cla<u>ss</u>   fu<u>ll</u>   ha<u>pp</u>y   stu<u>ff</u>   si<u>ll</u>y

Add the two consonant letters. Write a list word.

1. fu___ ___ _____

2. hi___ ___ _____

3. dre___ ___ _____

4. ha___ ___y _____

5. sha___ ___ _____

6. si___ ___y _____

7. stu___ ___ _____

8. cla___ ___ _____

Add the second consonant letter. Write a new word.

9. glas___ _____

10. of___ _____

11. fel___ _____

12. kis___ _____

13. ap___le _____ʼ __

14. chil___ _____

15. pas___ _____

16. cros___ _____

17. sum___er _____

18. bos___ _____

19. bal___ _____

20. pul___ _____

21. les___ _____

22. clif___ _____

23. ham___er _____

24. sup___er _____

25. rab___it _____

26. hel___o _____

27. bot___om _____

28. but___on _____

Score: / 28

D Proofread and Write

Here is a list of safety rules for a shop. It has three spelling mistakes. Draw a line through each misspelled word. Write the word correctly above it.

SAFETY RULES

Do not leave rags and other stuff on the floor.

Workers must go to a safety class every year.

Everyone shaell wear thick work shoes.

Make a ful report of any injury.

Stay alert! Don't make sily mistakes.

A safe shop is a happy shop.

Make a list of safety rules for your home or job. Use at least three list words.

_____

_____

_____

_____

_____

_____

_____

_____

Writing Folder

Proofread your list. Correct any mistakes. Then make a clean copy and put it in your writing folder.

18 Vowels Before *R*

Ⓐ Check the Meaning

Word List			
dark	store	shirt	car
yard	short	park	girl

Write the missing list word.

1. Clothes for a small _____ do not need to cost a lot of money. Shop wisely.

2. First find a _____ that has good prices. This may take time.

3. The same _____ can cost half the price at some stores.

4. It might save money to drive your _____ several miles for a sale.

5. If it is a big sale, get there early. If you drive, allow time to _____.

6. Buy clothes with room for a child to grow. A pair of pants can become too _____ quickly.

7. Clothes with _____ colors do not show dirt.

8. Buy clothes with many uses. Some things can be worn to school and to play in your _____.

Add two more sentences. Use at least one list word in each sentence.

9. _____

   _____

10. _____

   _____

Score: /10

B Study the Spelling

Add the missing letters. Then write the list word.

1. s___o___e _____

2. p___r___ _____

3. g___ ___l _____

4. ___hir___ _____

5. ya___ ___ _____

Write a list word for each of these clues.

6. It has only three letters. _____

7. They are the two list words that rhyme.

   _____ _____

8. It rhymes with *card.* _____

9. They begin with *sh.* _____ _____

10. They begin with two consonants.

   _____ _____ _____

One word in each group has a spelling mistake. Circle the word with the mistake. Then write it correctly.

11. park   yard   stoer   _____

12. gril   store   yard   _____

13. car   dork   short   _____

14. shoart   girl   shirt   _____

15. shirt   kar   dark   _____

C Build Your Skills

Spelling Tutor

R changes the sound of the vowel before it. Look at each word to remember how the sound is spelled.

dark	park
girl	shirt
short	store

Add the missing vowel. Write a list word.

1. c___r _____

2. st___re _____

3. y___rd _____

4. sh___rt _____

5. sh___rt _____

6. p___rk _____

7. g___rl _____

8. d___rk _____

Add an *a* before the *r*. Write a new word.

9. f___r _____

10. ___rt _____

11. h___rd _____

12. p___rty _____

13. st___rt _____

14. b___rn _____

Add an *i* before the *r*. Write a new word.

15. b___rd _____

16. d___rt _____

17. th___rsty _____

18. f___rst _____

Add an *o* before the r. Write a new word.

19. m___re _____

20. h___rse _____

21. h___rn _____

22. m___rning _____

Score: ___ / 22

Ⓓ Proofread and Write

Omar made the shopping list below. He made three spelling mistakes. Draw a line through each misspelled word. Write the word correctly above it.

Shopping List

Find a store with a sale.

Get a dark shert for Carl.

Buy shoes I can wear to the paerk.

Find socks for the gril next door.

Take back the pants I got last week. They are too short.

Put gas in the car.

Make your own shopping list. Use at least three list words.

_____

_____

_____

_____

Writing Folder

Proofread your shopping list. Correct any mistakes. Make a clean copy and put it in your writing folder.

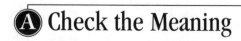

19 Words That Sound Alike

Ⓐ Check the Meaning

Word List

buy	hear	hole	sea
by	here	whole	see

Each pair of words in the word list sounds the same. They do not have the same meaning. Write the missing list word. The missing word sounds the same as the underlined word. It does not have the same meaning.

1. Did you <u>hear</u> the news? The meeting is going to be held

_____.

2. Please sit <u>here</u>. You will be able to _____ us better.

3. Go <u>by</u> the candy store. I want to _____ some gumdrops.

4. I need to <u>buy</u> a few eggs. Let's drive _____ the farm store.

5. From the roof of my house I can <u>see</u> the _____.

6. I wish I could _____ the <u>sea</u> more often.

7. It took the <u>whole</u> day to fill the _____ with dirt.

8. A small <u>hole</u> will make your _____ tire flat.

Write two more sentences. Use at least one pair of words in each sentence.

9. _____

_____

10. _____

_____

B Study the Spelling

Add the missing letters. Write the list words.

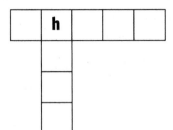
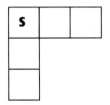
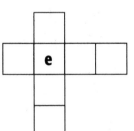

1._____

2._____

3._____

4._____

5._____

6._____

7._____

8._____

If the underlined word is misspelled, write it correctly. If it is correct, write C.

9. I want to <u>sea</u> the film. _____

10. Did you eat the <u>whole</u> hot dog? _____

11. I did not <u>here</u> the bell. _____

12. Ken will <u>by</u> the food. _____

13. I have a <u>hole</u> in my cap. _____

14. The ship is at <u>sea</u>. _____

15. Try to be <u>here</u> by noon. _____

Score: ___/15

Ⓒ Build Your Skills

Spelling Tutor

Some words sound the same, but they do not have the same spelling or meaning. The underlined words sound the same. They have different meanings.

Meg wore a <u>plain</u> black dress. I took a <u>plane</u> to New York.
I <u>rode</u> to work with Jim. The <u>road</u> was bumpy.
Cook the <u>meat</u> over the fire. The club will <u>meet</u> today.
She was <u>too</u> tired to play. I will see you in <u>two</u> days.
Give the award <u>to</u> Helen.
I <u>knew</u> the answer. We need a <u>new</u> table.

Choose the word that fits the sentence. Write it on the line.

1. I will (meat; meet) you at six o'clock. _____

2. We were served (plane; plain) hamburgers. _____

3. Do not add (too; two; to) much salt. _____

4. The (road; rode) led to the woods. _____

5. Is that a (new; knew) watch? _____

6. The (meat; meet) had spoiled. _____

7. Our (plane; plain) was an hour late. _____

8. Fran (road; rode) the bus to work. _____

9. No one (new; knew) the answer. _____

10. I ate (too; two; to) apples for lunch. _____

11. A sailor must know how (too; two; to) swim. _____

12. The store wrapped the gift in (plane; plain) white paper.

_____

Score: /12

D Proofread and Write

Edna left this note for Juan. She made three spelling mistakes. Draw a line through each misspelled word. Write the word correctly above it.

Juan,

Your mom came here to sea you

today. She will come buy again later.

She could not wait the hole day.

Did you hear the news? Jim fell in a

hole and hurt his leg.

Edna

Write a note to a friend or someone in your family. Use at least three list words.

_____

_____

_____

_____

_____

Writing Folder

Proofread your note. Correct any mistakes. Make a clean copy and put it in your writing folder.

20 Compound Words

Ⓐ Check the Meaning

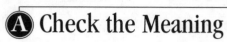

Word List

cannot	without	someone	myself
daylight	weekend	nobody	maybe

Write the missing list word.

1. Twice a year we change our clocks. This gives us more
   _____ on summer evenings.

2. I _____ always recall how to change the hands.

3. I need _____ to tell me if the clock moves ahead
   or back.

4. The change is made on a _____.

5. _____ this is because most people do not go to work then.

6. In some warm spots the clocks do not change. _____
   wants more hot sunshine.

7. Even _____ changing the clocks, the sun stays out
   longer in summer.

8. I change our clocks _____. This way I know it has
   been done right.

Add two more sentences. Use at least one list word in each sentence.

9. _____

   _____

10. _____

   _____

Score: /10

B Study the Spelling

Replace the underlined letters. Write a list word.

1. some<u>body</u> _____

2. <u>some</u>body _____

3. <u>sun</u>light _____

4. <u>your</u>self _____

5. week<u>day</u> _____

Write the list word or words for each clue.

6. It has eight letters. _____

7. It would come first in the dictionary. _____

8. It would come last in the dictionary. _____

9. These two words begin with *m*.

   _____ _____

10. The word *can* is part of this word. _____

Add the missing letters. Write the word.

11. with___ ___ ___   _____

12. ___ ___ ___ ___end   _____

13. may___ ___   _____

14. ___ ___ ___light   _____

Write the list word that fits each shape.

15.

16.

C Build Your Skills

Spelling Tutor

A compound word is made by putting two words together.
day + light = daylight
week + end = weekend

Write the two words that make up each list word.

1. _____ + _____ = daylight

2. _____ + _____ = weekend

3. _____ + _____ = maybe

4. _____ + _____ = cannot

5. _____ + _____ = myself

6. _____ + _____ = nobody

7. _____ + _____ = someone

8. _____ + _____ = without

Put the two words together. Write a new compound word.

9. pea + nut = _____

10. any + one = _____

11. bed + room = _____

12. in + side = _____

13. note + book = _____

14. every + where = _____

15. book + case = _____

16. base + ball = _____

17. birth + day = _____

18. him + self = _____

19. air + plane = _____

20. camp + fire = _____

Score: / 20

Ⓓ Proofread and Write

Julia read this story in a newspaper. She found three spelling mistakes. Find
the mistakes. Draw a line through each misspelled word. Then write the word
correctly above it.

Change Clocks Tonight!

Do you want more daylit? This is
the weekend to get it. You canot
get more sun without changing
your clocks. Move the time ahead
one hour. Maybe you will want to put this story by
a clock. It will remind you to change the time.
Nobudy is perfect.

Writing Folder

Write a short news story or report on another piece of paper. It can be
about anything that interests you. Use at least three list words.

Proofread your news story. Correct any mistakes. Make a clean copy
and put it in your writing folder.

Unit 5 Review

Finish the Meaning

Find the missing word. Fill in the circle.

1. Carlos goes to work very early in the morning. Sometimes, it is still _____ out.

   ○ silly
   ○ big
   ○ dark

2. Tina lost her keys outside in the _____.

   ○ yard
   ○ store
   ○ class

3. Tim needs clothes for a new job. Most of all he needs a _____.

   ○ box
   ○ shirt
   ○ flag

4. Ben is glad he brought a map. He could not find the street _____ it.

   ○ of
   ○ by
   ○ without

5. Liz has too much to do. The day always seems so _____.

   ○ stuck
   ○ short
   ○ funny

6. Ken must empty the trash. The trash can is _____.

   ○ full
   ○ wide
   ○ open

7. Jeff is going to work. He will _____ in business clothes.

   ○ dress
   ○ park
   ○ see

8. Sue is a very good student. She is the best in her _____.
   ○ rain
   ○ car
   ○ class

9. Please do not help me with this job. I want to do it _____.

   ○ myself
   ○ maybe
   ○ funny

10. Janet really wants to win the race. If she wins, she will be very _____.

    ○ even
    ○ happy
    ○ cold

GO ON ➡️

Check the Spelling

11. We will never fit all that
_____ into this box!

- ○ stuf
- ○ stuff
- ○ stof

12. Joe and Sara have two children,
one boy and one _____.

- ○ gril
- ○ girl
- ○ gerl

13. Joan will need a _____ to
get to her new job.

- ○ kar
- ○ cor
- ○ car

14. Summer brings many more hours
of _____.

- ○ daylite
- ○ daylight
- ○ deylight

15. Watch out! Do not fall into that
big _____!

- ○ hol
- ○ hole
- ○ hoal

16. I will have to find _____ to
help me move the sofa.

- ○ sumone
- ○ someone
- ○ somewon

17. I cannot _____ the music.

- ○ here
- ○ hear
- ○ heer

18. We can see the river from the top
of the _____.

- ○ hil
- ○ hile
- ○ hill

19. This _____ I will ride my
bike to the park.

- ○ weakend
- ○ weeken
- ○ weekend

20. Grandma makes the best apple pie.
_____ makes a better one!

- ○ Nobody
- ○ Nobuddy
- ○ Nobaudy

STOP

21 Question Words

A Check the Meaning

Word List

how	which	whose	what
when	who	why	where

Write the missing list word.

1. I have a boy and a girl. _____ many children do you have?

2. I cannot find my pen. _____ do you think it is? Could it be in the desk?

3. We do not want to be late. Our bus leaves at 10:04. _____ time is it now?

4. The books on the table are mine. _____ books are those? Are they your books?

5. I am lost without a map. _____ road should I take to town?

6. I am getting very hungry. _____ will lunch be ready? I hope it is soon.

7. The game will be very close. _____ do you think will win? I hope it is our team.

8. It will be very warm today. _____ did you wear a coat?

Add two more sentences. Use two list words.

9. _____

_____

10. _____

_____

Score: /10

B Study the Spelling

Write the missing letters in each puzzle. Then write the list word.

1. _____

2. _____

3. _____

4. _____

5. _____

   _____

6. _____

   _____

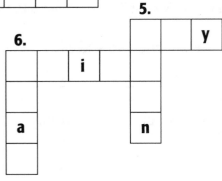

One word in each group is misspelled. Circle the misspelled word. Write it correctly.

7. what   whan   who   _____

8. whoze   why   which   _____

9. how   whare   why   _____

10. whut   what   when   _____

Write the list words with five letters. Circle the vowels.

11. _____   13. _____

12. _____

Write the list words with three letters. Circle the words that begin with *wh*.

14. _____   16. _____

15. _____

C Build Your Skills

Spelling Tutor

The first word in a sentence always begins with a capital letter. If the sentence makes a statement, it ends with a period. If it asks a question, it ends with a question mark.

The store is having a sale on milk.   Four boys went to the movie.
How much does the milk cost?   What did they see?

Copy each sentence. Add capital letters, periods, and question marks.

1. where are the tools kept

_____

2. she starts her new job today

_____

3. can you read the words on the sign

_____

4. try to eat fresh fruit every day

_____

5. how did the dish get broken

_____

6. everyone came to the meeting on safety

_____

7. never pay for things you did not order

_____

8. where did you find the stamps

_____

Score: ___ / 8

Ⓓ Proofread and Write

These are the questions Tao asked her babysitter. She made three spelling mistakes. She also forgot a question mark. Draw a line through each misspelled word. Write the word correctly above it. Add the question mark.

Questions for the Sitter

- Who could tell me about your work?

- Whan would you be able to begin work?

- Wat would you do in case of a fire

- How much do you charge for taking care of one baby?

- Where did you learn to care for a child?

- Whoze phone numbers do you want to have?

Make a list of questions you want to ask someone. It might be your doctor, a friend, or your boss. Use at least three list words. Be sure to use a question mark at the end of a question.

_____

_____

_____

_____

 Writing Folder

Proofread your list. Correct any mistakes. Make a clean copy and put it in your writing folder.

Family Words

Ⓐ Check the Meaning

> **Word List**
>
> | sister | mother | husband | daughter |
> |--------|--------|---------|----------|
> | brother | father | aunt | grandmother |

Write the missing list word.

1. I have always called my _____ Mom. She likes that better than Ma.

2. My _____ does not like being called Dad. I have always called him Pop.

3. I have a baby _____ named Sid. I think he is Mom's pet.

4. My older _____ is named Mary. She lives in the city.

5. Mary was Mom and Pop's first _____. I was their second.

6. Mary's _____ is named Sam. Sam and Mary have been married for a year.

7. Pop's sister is my _____. She comes over to see us almost every week.

8. Mom's mother is my _____. She is the oldest one in our family.

Add two more sentences. Use two list words.

9. _____

   _____

10. _____

   _____

Score: ⟋ 10

B Study the Spelling

Write the list word or words for each clue.

1. It has four letters and two vowels. _____

2. It has three syllables. _____

3. It has the word *band* in it. _____

4. They end with *ter*. _____ _____

5. It is made from two smaller words. _____

6. They have a *th* in their spelling. _____

_____

_____

_____

Add the missing letters. Write the word.

7. da___g___ter _____

8. b___o___ ___er _____

9. husb___ ___d _____

10. m___th___r _____

11. a___nt _____

12. gr___ndmo___ ___er _____

Write the list words in alphabetical order.

13. _____ 17. _____

14. _____ 18. _____

15. _____ 19. _____

16. _____ 20. _____

Score: ☐/20

C Build Your Skills

Spelling Tutor

A person's name always begins with a capital letter.

The name of an exact place or thing also begins with a capital letter.

I have an aunt in another city.   My <u>A</u>unt <u>B</u>eth lives in <u>M</u>emphis.
Some people live near the water.   <u>B</u>ob and <u>S</u>ue live on <u>C</u>ape <u>C</u>od <u>B</u>ay.

Copy each sentence. Add the capital letters where needed.

1. give the book to uncle fred.

_____

2. does lucy go to school yet?

_____

3. i hope to see you in new york.

_____

4. ask glen to join us at the beach.

_____

5. it costs fifty cents to cross monroe bridge.

_____

6. no one wants to go to war.

_____

7. the civil war cost many lives.

_____

8. we will meet on spring street.

_____

Score: / 8

Ⓓ Proofread and Write

Here is a letter about a family picnic. The writer made three spelling
mistakes. He also forgot to use three capital letters. Draw a line through each
misspelled word. Also draw a line through each word that needs a capital
letter. Write the word correctly above it.

67 Babb Avenue
Skokie, IL 60067
June 30, 1997

Dear Rosa,

I hope you can come to the family picnic. Our sister julia will

be there with her huzband. Aunt Sue said she would bring her

dauter. Grandmother is coming from batesville. Mother and

fathar will be sad if you do not show up.

Let me know your plans soon.

Your brother,

Carlos

 Writing Folder

Write a letter to someone. Use your own paper. Tell about your
family. Use at least three list words. Proofread your letter and correct
any mistakes. Mail your letter or keep it in your writing folder.

Food Words

Ⓐ Check the Meaning

Word List			
cake	bread	apple	grapes
eggs	bacon	sandwich	soup

Write the missing list word.

1. The farm stand has a sale on _____ today. You can buy two bunches for a dollar.

2. I love a bowl of hot _____ on a cold day. It really warms me up.

3. Every year we have _____ on Alicia's birthday. This year we did not put candles on it.

4. After dinner we had _____ pie and tea on the porch.

5. Josh got a dozen _____ at the store. He broke one on the way home.

6. Takita always takes a ham _____ to work. She has milk with it for lunch.

7. I love the smell of _____ as it bakes. I like to bake on the weekend.

8. I often wake up to the smell of _____ frying in the kitchen.

Add two more sentences. Use two list words.

9. _____

_____

10. _____

_____

Score: / 10

B Study the Spelling

Write the list word or words for each clue.

1. They have double letters in their spelling.

_____ _____

2. They end with *s* or *es* and mean "more than one."

_____ _____

3. They begin with two consonants.

_____ _____

4. It has the vowel sound you hear in *food*. It is spelled *ou*.

_____

5. It rhymes with *make*. _____

6. It rhymes with *head*. _____

7. They begin with a vowel.

_____ _____

Write the words with two syllables. Draw a line between the syllables.

8. _____   **10.** _____

9. _____

Write these list words in alphabetical order.

bacon   soup   bread   eggs

11. _____   **13.** _____

12. _____   **14.** _____

Add the missing letters. Write the list words.

15. san___wi___ ___   _____

16. ___gg___   _____

Ⓒ Build Your Skills

Spelling Tutor

Some words have silent letters. You may not hear these letters when you say the word. These letters are needed in spelling.

sand<u>d</u>wich   ma<u>t</u>ch   <u>k</u>not   <u>w</u>rite

Copy the sentences. Add the silent letters.

1. I fell and got a scra___ch on my ___nee.

_____

2. The workers ___new how to pa___ch the hole in the road.

_____

3. ___rap it in paper and tie it with a ___not.

_____

4. Twist the ___nob on the door with your ___rist.

_____

5. Never pi___ch a ___nife at anyone.

_____

6. Try not to ___nock the ___rench off the bench.

_____

7. He will ___nit some socks and a ma___ching tie.

_____

8. They must wa___ch the game and ___rite a report.

_____

_____

Score: ___ / 8

Ⓓ Proofread and Write

This is Tim's shopping list. He made four spelling mistakes. Draw a line through each misspelled word. Write the word correctly above it.

Shopping List

6 eggs

1 loaf of white bred

1 pound of bacon

sanwich meat

appel pie

1 bag of grapes

4 cans of soop

cake mix

Make your own shopping list. Use at least four list words.

_____

_____

_____

_____

_____

_____

Writing Folder

Proofread your list. Correct any mistakes. Make a clean copy and put it in your writing folder.

Color Words

A Check the Meaning

Word List			
brown	pink	white	gray
green	red	blue	yellow

Write the missing list word.

1. The lake was no longer clear. The rain had turned the water a muddy _____ color.

2. The butter turned the popcorn a golden _____. It even smelled better.

3. The grass seemed to be dying. After the shower, however, the grass became a bright _____.

4. There are fifty stars in the U.S. flag. They are placed on a _____ background.

5. Wait until the apples are ripe. Do not pick any that have not turned _____.

6. The stars looked like small, _____ lights in the dark sky.

7. His kind words made me blush. I felt my cheeks turning _____.

8. My father is almost sixty years of age. His hair has become quite _____.

Add two more sentences. Use two list words.

9. _____

_____

10. _____

_____

Score: ___ / 10

B Study the Spelling

Write the list word or words for each of these clues.

1. They begin with *gr*. _____

   _____

2. It ends with a long a sound spelled *ay*. _____

3. It rhymes with *true*. _____

4. It is a two-syllable word. _____

5. It rhymes with *think*. _____

6. It begins with *wh*. _____

Replace the underlined letters. Write a list word.

7. <u>f</u>rown _____

8. <u>b</u>ed _____

9. <u>s</u>ink _____

10. <u>q</u>uite _____

11. <u>m</u>ellow _____

12. <u>qu</u>een _____

13. gr<u>im</u> _____

14. blu<u>r</u> _____

Write the missing letters in each puzzle. Then write the list word.

15. _____

16. _____

   _____

17. _____

18. _____

19. _____

20. _____

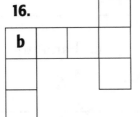

C Build Your Skills

Spelling Tutor

Sometimes two consonants blend together. When they do, the separate sounds may be hard to hear. Sometimes two consonants make a new sound. Always note the spelling of the two consonants.

white	green	brown	blue	spin
church	ship	thin	those	clip

Copy each sentence. Add the two missing consonants.

1. The huge ___ ___ip moved through the sea. Nobody had to tou___ ___ the wheel.

   _____

   _____

2. I love fried ___ ___icken and potatoes with ___ ___own ___ ___avy.

   _____

   _____

3. Be sure to ___ ___ew your food. Do not ___ ___ill food on your ___ ___ouse.

   _____

   _____

4. For dinner we ate a ___ ___ick hamburger. I had a slice of ___ ___eese on mine.

   _____

   _____

5. I hate to ___ ___ave every day. I often cut my ___ ___in with the blade.

   _____

   _____

Score: /5

Ⓓ Proofread and Write

Elena filled out this order for clothes. She made three spelling mistakes. Draw
a line through each misspelled word. Write the word correctly above it.

THE CLOTHING WAREHOUSE, ORDER FORM

Name: Elena Wagner
Address: 112 Topper St.
Mesa, AZ 85213

Catalog Number	Item	Quantity	Size	Color	Unit Cost	Total
03566	wool socks	4	large	blew	$2.00	$8.00
49877	hat	1	medium	red	$15.00	$15.00
97621	gloves	2	small	green	$12.00	$24.00
65766	shirt	1	large	wite	$22.00	$22.00
32309	blouse	2	medium	gray	$10.00	$20.00
44848	coat	1	large	broun	$45.00	$45.00
					Total	**$134.00**

Write an order for some clothes. Give the item, size, and color you want. Use
at least four list words.

Item	Size	Color

Writing Folder

Proofread your order. Correct any mistakes. Make a clean copy and put it in
your writing folder.

Unit 6 Review

Finish the Meaning

Find the missing word. Fill in the circle.

1. Cindy needs to change the oil in her car. Mary will show her _____ to do it.
   - ○ who
   - ○ which
   - ○ how

2. We had lots of rain this spring. The grass has never been so _____.
   - ○ blue
   - ○ black
   - ○ green

3. Do you want pizza for lunch? No, I want a bowl of hot _____ instead.
   - ○ snack
   - ○ soup
   - ○ bread

4. Her dress is the color of the U.S. flag: red, white, and _____.
   - ○ pink
   - ○ yellow
   - ○ blue

5. The diner gives you a choice of meat. You can have ham or _____.
   - ○ bacon
   - ○ milk
   - ○ fish

6. How many candles did she have on her birthday _____?
   - ○ plate
   - ○ cake
   - ○ wish

7. We are lucky to have such a good hen. She always lays plenty of _____.
   - ○ eggs
   - ○ grapes
   - ○ lunch

8. Shing likes everyone in his family. His mother's sister, Chun, is his favorite _____.
   - ○ father
   - ○ aunt
   - ○ brother

9. Clara is having a baby in June. She will be a very good _____.
   - ○ man
   - ○ mother
   - ○ husband

10. Tom always puts his glasses on the table. Then he always knows _____ to find them.
    - ○ where
    - ○ were
    - ○ whose

GO ON ➡

Check the Spelling

Choose the word that is spelled correctly and best completes the sentence.

11. That shirt is filthy! It will never be _____ again.
    - ○ white
    - ○ whit
    - ○ whyte
    - ○ wite

12. Nana always brings treats. She is a perfect _____.
    - ○ granmother
    - ○ grandmuther
    - ○ grandmother
    - ○ grandmather

13. Do you want ice cream on your _____ pie?
    - ○ aple
    - ○ apple
    - ○ appel
    - ○ apel

14. Kathy and Dave have two sons and one _____.
    - ○ daghter
    - ○ dauter
    - ○ dawter
    - ○ daughter

15. Carl eats the same thing every day: a peanut butter and jelly _____.
    - ○ sandwich
    - ○ sandwech
    - ○ sanwich
    - ○ sandwish

16. I want to be on time for the movie. _____ does it start?
    - ○ When
    - ○ Wen
    - ○ Whin
    - ○ Wenn

17. Sam was in the sun too long. His nose is very _____.
    - ○ read
    - ○ red
    - ○ rad
    - ○ wred

18. Tony's boss wants to know _____ the report is late.
    - ○ why
    - ○ wie
    - ○ wye
    - ○ wigh

19. Are your eyes blue, green, or _____?
    - ○ browne
    - ○ braun
    - ○ broun
    - ○ brown

20. Show your children _____ to do in case of fire.
    - ○ wat
    - ○ whut
    - ○ what
    - ○ wut

STOP

How to Study a Word

1 **Look**
at the word.

2 **Say**
the word aloud.

3 **Cover**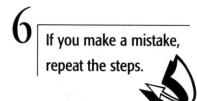
the word.

4 **Write**
the word.

5 **Check**
the spelling.

6 If you make a mistake,
repeat the steps.

Personal Word List

Write any words that need more study. You can write words you see in this book, at work, or at home.

_____	_____	_____
_____	_____	_____
_____	_____	_____
_____	_____	_____
_____	_____	_____
_____	_____	_____
_____	_____	_____
_____	_____	_____
_____	_____	_____
_____	_____	_____
_____	_____	_____

Personal Word List

Write any words that need more study. You can write words you see in this book, at work, or at home.

Alphabetical Word List

Word	Lesson	Word	Lesson	Word	Lesson
any	12	eat	14	job	8
apple	23	eggs	23	jump	9
are	12	even	10	just	9
aunt	22	every	16	kick	15
bacon	23	fast	5	kind	11
best	6	father	22	knock	8
big	7	find	11	lake	13
black	15	fish	7	lid	7
blind	11	flag	5	love	16
blue	24	float	14	lunch	9
boat	14	flop	8	make	13
box	8	friend	16	man	5
bread	23	full	17	many	16
bring	7	funny	9	map	5
brother	22	gas	5	maybe	20
brown	24	get	6	milk	7
buy	19	girl	18	most	11
by	19	go	10	mother	22
cake	23	got	8	must	9
cannot	20	grandmother	22	myself	20
car	18	grapes	23	nobody	20
cash	5	gray	24	nose	13
child	11	green	24	of	16
class	17	happy	17	only	10
cold	11	hat	5	open	10
come	12	have	16	park	18
cup	9	he	10	pen	6
dark	18	hear	19	pick	15
daughter	22	here	19	pink	24
daylight	20	hill	17	plate	13
did	7	hold	11	play	14
dock	15	hole	19	rain	14
does	12	how	21	ran	5
dress	17	husband	22	red	24

Word	Lesson	Word	Lesson
ride	13	very	12
rock	15	was	16
run	9	we	10
said	12	weekend	20
sandwich	23	went	6
sea	19	were	12
see	19	wet	6
send	6	what	21
shall	17	when	21
she	10	where	21
shirt	18	which	21
shock	8	white	24
short	18	who	21
show	14	whole	19
sick	15	whose	21
silly	17	why	21
sister	22	wide	13
sleep	14	win	7
snack	15	wish	7
so	10	without	20
sold	11	yard	18
someone	20	yellow	24
soup	23	yes	6
spot	8	you	12
stick	15		
stop	8		
store	18		
stuck	9		
stuff	17		
them	6		
these	13		
they	16		
trail	14		
use	13		

Handwriting Models

D'Nealian™ Manuscript Alphabet

a b c d e f g h i j k l m

n o p q r s t u v w x y z

A B C D E F G

H I J K L M N O P Q

R S T U V W X Y Z

D'Nealian™ Cursive Alphabet

a b c d e f g h i j k

l m n o p q r s t

u v w x y z . . ? " " !

A B C D E F G H I

J K L M N O P Q R

S T U V W X Y Z

D'Nealian™ Numbers

1 2 3 4 5 6 7 8 9 10

The Vowels and Consonants

The Vowels

Aa	as in	**c<u>a</u>t**		**Oo**	as in	**h<u>o</u>t**
Ee	as in	**b<u>e</u>d**		**Uu**	as in	**f<u>u</u>n**
Ii	as in	**p<u>i</u>n**		**Yy**	as in	**sk<u>y</u>**

The Consonants

Bb	as in	**<u>b</u>ig**		**Pp**	as in	**<u>p</u>eg**
Cc	as in	**<u>c</u>ap**		**Qq**	as in	**<u>q</u>uack**
Dd	as in	**<u>d</u>og**		**Rr**	as in	**<u>r</u>ag**
Ff	as in	**<u>f</u>ish**		**Ss**	as in	**<u>s</u>it**
Gg	as in	**<u>g</u>ame**		**Tt**	as in	**<u>t</u>op**
Hh	as in	**<u>h</u>elp**		**Vv**	as in	**<u>v</u>an**
Jj	as in	**<u>j</u>ar**		**Ww**	as in	**<u>w</u>ig**
Kk	as in	**<u>k</u>ite**		**Xx**	as in	**bo<u>x</u>**
Ll	as in	**<u>l</u>ip**		**Yy**	as in	**<u>y</u>ard**
Mm	as in	**<u>m</u>ap**		**Zz**	as in	**<u>z</u>ebra**
Nn	as in	**<u>n</u>ap**				

Answer Key

Unit 1, Lesson 1
Page 10: 1. sailboat, **2.** monkey, **3.** tree, **4.** pen, **5.** nest
Page 11: 1. m, **2.** p, **3.** t, **4.** s, **5.** n, **6.** m, **7.** p, **8.** t, **9.** n, **10.** s
Page 12: 1. p, pin; **2.** s, sun; **3.** m, man; **4.** n, nail; **5.** t, ten; **6.** t, tree; **7.** s, saw; **8.** n, nine; **9.** m, mouth; **10.** p, pizza
Page 13: 1. p, map; **2.** t, cat; **3.** s, bus; **4.** n, fan; **5.** m, drum; **6.** n, can; **7.** t, net; **8.** p, cap; **9.** n, barn; **10.** s, plus

Unit 1, Lesson 2
Page 14: 1. lamp, **2.** kite, **3.** rake, **4.** bus, **5.** jug
Page 15: 1. r, **2.** k, **3.** b, **4.** j, **5.** l, **6.** k, **7.** r, **8.** b, **9.** l, **10.** r
Page 16: 1. l, leg; **2.** r, ring; **3.** b, bird; **4.** k, kite; **5.** j, jet; **6.** b, book; **7.** l, lips; **8.** r, rope; **9.** j, jacks; **10.** k, king
Page 17: 1. b, web; **2.** r, chair; **3.** l, bell; **4.** k, cook; **5.** b, tub; **6.** r, bear; **7.** l, snail; **8.** k, fork; **9.** l, girl; **10.** b, bib

Unit 1, Lesson 3
Page 18: 1. fish, **2.** glasses, **3.** house, **4.** desk, **5.** woman
Page 19: 1. d, **2.** w, **3.** h, **4.** f, **5.** g, **6.** f, **7.** g, **8.** d, **9.** g, **10.** d
Page 20: 1. w, web; **2.** h, hat; **3.** g, gun; **4.** d, door; **5.** f, fan; **6.** d, dish; **7.** f, fire; **8.** w, worm; **9.** g, goat; **10.** h, hand
Page 21: 1. f, roof; **2.** g, flag; **3.** d, bread; **4.** g, frog; **5.** d, sled; **6.** f, shelf; **7.** d, bed; **8.** g, wig; **9.** f, leaf; **10.** p, pig

Unit 1, Lesson 4
Page 22: 1. vest, **2.** carrots, **3.** yarn, **4.** zipper, **5.** queen
Page 23: 1. v, **2.** c, **3.** y, **4.** z, **5.** q, **6.** z, **7.** v, **8.** y, **9.** c, **10.** q
Page 24: 1. v, van; **2.** c, camel; **3.** y, yo-yo; **4.** z, zipper; **5.** q, quarter; **6.** c, cow; **7.** y, yarn; **8.** v, vest; **9.** q, queen; **10.** z, zebra

Page 25: 1. q, equal; **2.** v, stove; **3.** y, lawyer; **4.** q, square; **5.** c, fact; **6.** z, quiz; **7.** y, year; **8.** v, seven; **9.** c, act; **10.** z, lazy

Unit 1 Review
Page 26: 1. glasses, **2.** rake, **3.** carrots, **4.** worm, **5.** quarter, **6.** fish, **7.** jug, **8.** lamp
Page 27: 9. d, **10.** r, **11.** s, **12.** m, **13.** p, **14.** v, **15.** f, **16.** l, **17.** r, **18.** t, **19.** h, **20.** g, **21.** z, **22.** n, **23.** y, **24.** b, **25.** k, **26.** j, **27.** w, **28.** q

Unit 2, Lesson 5
Page 28: 1. man, **2.** gas, **3.** fast, **4.** hat, **5.** map, **6.** flag, **7.** ran, **8.** cash, **9–10.** Answers will vary.
Page 29: 1. fast, **2.** map, **3.** cash, **4.** flag, **5.** l, flag; **6.** s, cash; **7.** g, gas; **8.** n, ran; **9.** h, hat; **10.** n, man; **11–12.** ran, man, **13–15.** flag, fast, cash, **16.** ran, **17.** fast, **18.** ran, **19.** cash, **20.** man, **21.** flag, **22.** map, **23.** gas, **24.** hat
Page 30: 1. a, map; **2.** a, hat; **3.** a, fast; **4.** a, gas; **5.** a, ran; **6.** a, flag; **7.** bad, **8.** last, **9.** lap, **10.** pack, **11.** sack, **12.** stamp, **13.** back, **14.** dash, **15.** pan, **16.** cap, **17.** tap, **18.** crash, **19.** than, **20.** fat, **21.** rang, **22.** fan, **23.** tan, **24.** lamb, **25.** fan, **26.** patch, **27.** land, **28.** clamp
Page 31: fast, gas, flag

Unit 2, Lesson 6
Page 32: 1. yes, **2.** get, **3.** send, **4.** pen, **5.** them, **6.** went, **7.** wet, **8.** best, **9–10.** Answers will vary.
Page 33: 1. them, **2.** yes, **3.** send, **4.** went, **5.** get, **6.** wet, **7.** best, **8.** wet, **9.** best, **10.** went, **11.** pen, **12.** get, wet; **13.** yes, **14–17.** b(e)(st), s(e)(nd), th(e)(m), w(e)(nt), **18.** them, **19.** best, **20.** wet
Page 34: 1. e, best; **2.** e, wet; **3.** e, yes; **4.** e, pen; **5.** e, get; **6.** e, them; **7.** e, went; **8.** e, send; **9.** bend, **10.** net, **11.** set, **12.** end, **13.** bell, **14.** belt, **15.** met, **16.** ten, **17.** leg, **18.** rest, **19.** fell, **20.** desk, **21.** men, **22.** deck, **23.** bet, **24.** peck, **25.** bet, **26.** beg, **27.** set, **28.** bed, **29.** bend, **30.** send
Page 35: them, went, best

Unit 2, Lesson 7

Page 36: 1. win, **2.** bring, **3.** big, **4.** milk, **5.** wish, **6.** fish, **7.** lid, **8.** did, **9–10.** Answers will vary.

Page 37: 1. win, wish; **2.** milk, lid; **3.** big, bring; **4.** fish, wish; **5.** did, **6.** big, **7.** milk, **8.** lid, **9.** bring, **10–13.** (br)i(ng), (f)i(sh), (m)i(lk), (w)i(sh); **14.** did, lid; **15.** fish, wish

Page 38: 1. i, wish; **2.** i, big; **3.** i, fish; **4.** i, win; **5.** i, did; **6.** i, lid; **7.** i, milk; **8.** i, bring; **9.** i, hid; **10.** i, sit; **11.** i, dig; **12.** i, thin; **13.** i, blink; **14.** i, dim; **15.** i, pig; **16.** i, him; **17.** i, this; **18.** i, kiss; **19.** i, clip; **20.** i, drink; **21.** i, flip; **22.** i, print; **23.** i, city; **24.** i, brick; **25.** i, quiz; **26.** i, hill; **27.** i, sink; **28.** i, kick; **29.** i, limp; **30.** i, lip

Page 39: fish, bring, milk, win

Unit 2, Lesson 8

Page 40: 1. box, **2.** spot, **3.** knock, **4.** stop, **5.** shock, **6.** job, **7.** flop, **8.** got, **9–10.** Answers will vary.

Page 41: 1. flop, **2.** job, **3.** knock, **4.** shock, **5.** knock, **6.** box, **7.** stop, **8.** job, **9.** got, **10.** shock, **11.** stop, flop; **12.** shock, knock; **13.** lo, flop; **14.** h, k, shock; **15.** x, box; **16.** p, spot; **17.** t, stop; **18.** j, job; **19.** k, knock; **20.** t, got

Page 42: 1. o, box; **2.** o, stop; **3.** o, flop; **4.** o, job; **5.** o, shock; **6.** o, knock; **7.** o, spot; **8.** o, got; **9.** o, odd; **10.** o, chop; **11.** o, body; **12.** o, copy; **13.** o, jog; **14.** o, knot; **15.** o, fox; **16.** o, block; **17.** o, bomb; **18.** o, hot; **19.** o, shop; **20.** o, robin; **21.** o, comet; **22.** o, mop; **23.** o, rock; **24.** o, pocket; **25.** o, pond; **26.** o, hockey; **27.** o, lock; **28.** o, flock

Page 43: got, job, knock

Unit 2 Review

Page 44: 1. spot, **2.** knock, **3.** bring, **4.** best, **5.** flop, **6.** job, **7.** map, **8.** shock, **9.** them, **10.** stop, **11.** went, **12.** cash, **13.** send, **14.** flag, **15.** gas, **16.** fast, **17.** yes, **18.** wet

Unit 3, Lesson 9

Page 46: 1. must, **2.** lunch, **3.** jump, **4.** cup, **5.** just, **6.** stuck, **7.** funny, **8.** run, **9–10.** Answers will vary.

Page 47: 1. lunch, **2.** jump, **3.** cup, **4.** stuck, **5.** run, **6.** funny, **7–8.** just, must; **9.** funy, funny; **10.** stuk, stuck; **11.** lanch, lunch; **11.** runn, run; **12.** jump, **13.** must, **14.** just, **15.** cup

Page 48: 1. u, stuck; **2.** u, run; **3.** u, lunch; **4.** u, just; **5.** u, funny; **6.** u, cup; **7.** u, jump; **8.** u, must; **9.** u, drum; **10.** u, truck; **11.** u, such; **12.** u, sun; **13.** u, under; **14.** u, summer; **15.** u, Sunday; **16.** u, club; **17.** u, bus; **18.** u, up; **19.** u, mud; **20.** u, ugly

Page 49: lunch, must, just

Unit 3, Lesson 10

Page 50: 1. even, **2.** go, **3.** He, **4.** We, **5.** open, **6.** She, **7.** only, **8.** so, **9–10.** Answers will vary.

Page 51: 1–3. even, only, open, **4–7.** we, she, he, open, (also so), **8–9.** so, go, **10–12.** he, she, we, **13.** o(pen), **14.** s(he), **15.** (on)ly

Page 52: 1–8. (e)ven, g(o), h(e), (o)nly, (o)pen, sh(e), s(o), w(e), **9.** e, be; **10.** o, sofa; **11.** o, pony; **12.** e, below; **13.** e, equal; **14.** o, bonus; **15.** o, soda; **16.** e, being; **17.** e, between; **18.** o, fold; **19.** o, total; **20.** e, fever; **21.** e, evil; **22.** o, cozy; **23.** o, holy; **24.** o, motor; **25.** e, real; **26.** e, veto

Page 53: only, open, he, even

Unit 3, Lesson 11

Page 54: 1. cold, **2.** child, **3.** most, **4.** find, **5.** hold, **6.** sold, **7.** kind, **8.** blind, **9–10.** Answers will vary.

Page 55: 1. sold, **2–3.** cold, hold; **4.** find, **5–6.** kind, blind; **7.** m, most; **8.** d, hold; **9.** li, blind; **10.** h, l, child; **11.** n, kind; **12.** b, d, blind; **13.** c, d, child; **14.** in, find; **15.** ol, sold; **16.** child, blind; **17.** sold, **18.** kind, **19.** most, **20.** hold

Page 56: 1–8. ch(i)ld, c(o)ld, bl(i)nd, f(i)nd, m(o)st, k(i)nd, h(o)ld, s(o)ld, **9.** o, old; **10.** i, pint; **11.** o, scold; **12.** o, ghost; **13.** i, behind; **14.** i, grind; **15.** o, bold;

16. i, sign; 17. o, both; 18. o, bolt; 19. i, wind; 20. o, colt;
21. o, post; 22. i, climb; 23. o, gold; 24. i, wild
Page 57: find, child, kind

Unit 3, Lesson 12

Page 58: 1. very, 2. you, 3. any, 4. were, 5. does,
6. said, 7. come, 8. are, 9–10. Answers will vary.
Page 59: 1. r, are; 2. o, come; 3. ou, you; 4. e, e, were;
5. v, r, very; 6. o, s, does; 7. come, 8. are, 9. any, very;
10. said, 11. any, very; 12. you, 13. very, 14. said,
15. you, 16. any, 17. were, 18. does
Page 60: 1. b, 2. g, 3. k, 4. y, 5. n, 6. e, 7. v, 8. c, 9. p,
10. i, 11. s, 12. l, 13. box, fish, man, 14. boy, hop, job,
15. case, clip, glad; 16. dish, ship, such
Page 61: very, any, said

Unit 3 Review

Page 62: 1. funny, 2. sold, 3. child, 4. He, 5. said,
6. must, 7. lunch, 8. hold, 9. find, 10. any
Page 63: 11. does, 12. stuck, 13. even, 14. blind,
15. most, 16. cold, 17. kind, 18. you, 19. are, 20. come

Unit 4, Lesson 13

Page 64: 1. make, 2. lake, 3. nose, 4. wide, 5. plate,
6. use, 7. ride, 8. These, 9–10. Answers will vary.
Page 65: 1. lake, make; 2. nose, 3. plate, these;
4. ride, wide; 5. wide, 6. you, wide; 7. s, nose;
8. l, e, plate; 9. a, e, lake; 10. id, ride; 11. i, e, wide;
12. u, e, use; 13. these, 14. use, 15. wide
Page 66: 1–8. l(ake), m(ake), n(ose), pl(ate), r(ide),
th(ese), (use), w(ide), 9. a, e, gave; 10. a, e, save; 11. a, e,
plate; 12. a, e, name; 13. i, e, five; 14. i, e, size; 15. i, e,
crime; 16. i, e, side; 17. o, e, bone; 18. o, e, hope;
19. o, e, those; 20. o, e, stone
Page 67: plate, use, wide

Unit 4, Lesson 14

Page 68: 1. eat, 2. show, 3. sleep, 4. play, 5. rain,
6. float, 7. boat, 8. trail, 9–10. Answers will vary.

Page 69: 1. rain, 2. play, 3. boat, 4. trail, 5. show,
6. sleep, 7. eat, 8. play, 9. show, 10. trail, 11. sleep,
12–15. b(oa)t, pl(ay), r(ai)n, sh(ow); 16. (bote), boat;
17. (tral), trial; 18. (eet), eat; 19. play, 20. sleep
Page 70: 1–8. b(oa)t, e(at), fl(oa)t, pl(ay), r(ai)n, sh(ow),
sl(ee)p, tr(ai)l, 9. a, i, afraid, 10. a, subway, 11. o, w,
throw, 12. o, road, 13. e, cream, 14. o, snow,
15. e, e, keep; 16. o, bowl; 17. a, y, delay; 18 o, coach
Page 71: sleep, boat, trail

Unit 4, Lesson 15

Page 72: 1. pick, 2. dock, 3. kick, 4. rock, 5. snack,
6. stick, 7. black, 8. sick, 9–10. Answers will vary.
Page 73: 1. snack, 2. rock, 3. pick, 4. dock, 5. stick,
6–8. (bl)ack, (sn)ack, (st)ick, 9. c, kick; 10. i, c, sick;
11. l, k, black; 12. st, stick; 13. na, snack; 14. c, rock;
15. i, c, pick; 16. dock, rock; 17. kick, 18. stick,
19. rock, 20. stick,
Page 74: 1–8. bla(ck), ro(ck), do(ck), si(ck), ki(ck),
sna(ck), pi(ck), sti(ck), 9. ck, lock; 10. ck, clock; 11. ck,
thick; 12. ck, trick; 13. ck, neck; 14. ck, brick; 15. ck,
check; 16. ck, truck; 17. ck, speck; 18. ck, wreck;
Page 75: pick, snacks, sticks

Unit 4, Lesson 16

Page 76: 1. was, 2. love, 3. every, 4. many, 5. have,
6. they, 7. of, 8. friend, 9–10. Answers will vary.
Page 77: 1. of, 2. was, 3. friend, 4. many, 5. they,
6. love, 7. every, 8. have, 9. a, many; 10. o, love;
11. a, was; 12. a, have; 13. e, they; 14. many, 15. of,
16. friend, 17. they, 18. have, 19. was, 20. love
Page 78: 1. we have, 2. They are, 3. do not,
4. has not, 5. You will, 6. is not, 7. isn't, 8. Don't,
9. you'll, 10. We've, 11. hasn't 12. They're
Page 79: many, was, Every, have

Unit 4 Review

Page 80: 1. sleep, 2. sick, 3. plate, 4. friend, 5. snack,
6. wide, 7. Every, 8. dock, 9. float, 10. They

Page 81: 11. of, **12.** many, **13.** was, **14.** have, **15.** black, **16.** trail, **17.** nose, **18.** hill **19.** these **20.** pick

Unit 5, Lesson 17

Page 82: 1. class, **2.** silly, **3.** dress, **4.** full, **5.** stuff, **6.** hill, **7.** happy, **8.** shall, **9–10.** Answers will vary.
Page 83: 1. full, stuff; **2.** silly, happy; **3.** happy, hill; **4.** dress, **5.** full, hill; **6.** class, **7.** shall, **8–13.** class, dress, (happy), shall, (silly), stuff , **14.** shall, **15.** stuff, **16.** class, **17.** dress, **18.** hill, **19.** happy, **20.** silly
Page 84: 1. l, l, full; **2.** l, l, hill; **3.** s, s, dress; **4.** p, p, happy; **5.** l, l, shall; **6.** l, l, silly; **7.** f, f, stuff; **8.** s, s, class; **9.** s, glass; **10.** f, off; **11.** l, fell; **12.** s, kiss; **13.** p, apple; **14.** l, chill; **15.** s, pass; **16.** s, cross; **17.** m, summer; **18.** s, boss; **19.** l, ball; **20.** l, pull; **21.** s, less; **22.** f, cliff; **23.** m, hammer; **24.** p, supper; **25.** b, rabbit; **26.** l, hello; **27.** t, bottom; **28.** t, button
Page 85: shall, full, silly

Unit 5, Lesson 18

Page 86: 1. girl, **2.** store, **3.** shirt, **4.** car, **5.** park, **6.** short, **7.** dark, **8.** yard, **9–10.** Answers will vary.
Page 87: 1. t, r, store; **2.** a, k, park; **3.** i, r, girl; **4.** s, t, shirt; **5.** r, d, yard; **6.** car, **7.** dark, park; **8.** yard, **9.** short, shirt; **10.** store, short, shirt; **11.** (stoer), store; **12.** (gril), girl; **13.** (dork), dark; **14.** (shoart), short; **15.** (kar), car
Page 88: 1. a, car; **2.** o, store; **3.** a, yard; **4.** o, short; **5.** i, shirt; **6.** a, park; **7.** i, girl; **8.** a, dark; **9.** a, far; **10.** a, art; **11.** a, hard; **12.** a, party; **13.** a, start; **14.** a, barn; **15.** i, bird; **16.** i, dirt; **17.** i, thirsty; **18.** i, first; **19.** o, more; **20.** o, horse; **21.** o, horn; **22.** o, morning
Page 89: shirt, park, girl

Unit 5, Lesson 19

Page 90: 1. here, **2.** hear, **3.** buy, **4.** by, **5.** sea, **6.** see, **7.** hole, **8.** whole, **9–10.** Answers will vary.
Page 91: 1–2. buy, by; **3–4.** whole, hole; **5–6.** sea, see; **7–8.** hear, here; **9.** see, **10.** C, **11.** hear, **12.** buy, **13.** C, **14.** C, **15.** C

Page 92: 1. meet, **2.** plain, **3.** too, **4.** road, **5.** new, **6.** meat, **7.** plane, **8.** rode, **9.** knew, **10.** two, **11.** to, **12.** plain
Page 93: see, by, whole

Unit 5, Lesson 20

Page 94: 1. daylight, **2.** cannot, **3.** someone, **4.** weekend, **5.** Maybe, **6.** Nobody, **7.** without, **8.** myself, **9–10.** Answers will vary.
Page 95: 1. someone, **2.** nobody, **3.** daylight, **4.** myself, **5.** weekend, **6.** daylight, **7.** cannot, **8.** without, **9.** maybe, myself; **10.** cannot, **11.** o, u, t, without; **12.** w, e, e, k, weekend; **13.** b, e, maybe; **14.** d, a, y, daylight; **15.** maybe, **16.** cannot
Page 96: 1. day, light; **2.** week, end; **3.** may, be; **4.** can, not; **5.** my, self; **6.** no, body; **7.** some, one; **8.** with, out; **9.** peanut, **10.** anyone, **11.** bedroom, **12.** inside, **13.** notebook, **14.** everywhere, **15.** bookcase, **16.** baseball, **17.** birthday, **18.** himself, **19.** airplane, **20.** campfire
Page 97: daylight, cannot, Nobody

Unit 5 Review

Page 98: 1. dark, **2.** yard, **3.** shirt, **4.** without, **5.** short, **6.** full, **7.** dress, **8.** class, **9.** myself, **10.** happy
Page 99: 11. stuff, **12.** girl, **13.** car, **14.** daylight, **15.** hole, **16.** someone, **17.** hear, **18.** hill, **19.** weekend, **20.** Nobody

Unit 6, Lesson 21

Page 100: 1. How, **2.** Where, **3.** What, **4.** Whose, **5.** Which, **6.** When, **7.** Who, **8.** Why, **9–10.** Answers will vary.
Page 101: 1. who, **2.** how, **3.** whose, **4.** where, **5.** why, when; **6.** which, what; **7.** (whan), when; **8.** (whoze), whose; **9.** (whare), where; **10.** (whut), what; **11.** wh(e)r(e), **12.** wh(o)s(e), **13.** wh(i)ch, **14.** how, **15.** (wh)o, **16.** (wh)y,
Page 102: 1. Where are the tools kept? **2.** She starts her new job today. **3.** Can you read the words on

the sign? **4.** Try to eat fresh fruit every day. **5.** How did the dish get broken? **6.** Everyone came to the meeting on safety. **7.** Never pay for things you did not order. **8.** Where did you find the stamps?
Page 103: When, What do you do in case of fire?, Whose

Unit 6, Lesson 22

Page 104: 1. mother, **2.** father, **3.** brother, **4.** sister, **5.** daughter, **6.** husband, **7.** aunt, **8.** grandmother, **9–10.** Answers will vary.
Page 105: 1. aunt, **2.** grandmother, **3.** husband, **4.** sister, daughter; **5.** grandmother, **6.** brother, father; mother, grandmother; **7.** u, h, daughter; **8.** r, t, h, brother; **9.** b, a, husband; **10.** o, e, mother; **11.** u, aunt; **12.** a, t, h, grandmother **13–20.** aunt, brother, daughter, father, grandmother, husband, mother, sister
Page 106: 1. Give the book to Uncle Fred.
2. Does Lucy go to school yet? **3.** I hope to see you in New York. **4.** Ask Glen to join us at the beach.
5. It costs fifty cents to cross Monroe Bridge.
6. No one wants to go to war. **7.** The Civil War cost many lives. **8.** We will meet on Spring Street.
Page 107: Julia, husband, daughter, Batesville, Father

Unit 6, Lesson 23

Page 108: 1. grapes, **2.** soup, **3.** cake, **4.** apple, **5.** eggs, **6.** sandwich, **7.** bread, **8.** bacon, **9–10.** Answers will vary.
Page 109: 1. eggs, apple, **2.** eggs, grapes, **3.** bread, grapes, **4.** soup, **5.** cake, **6.** bread, **7.** eggs, apple, **8–10.** ba/con, ap/ple, sand/wich, **11.** bacon, **12.** bread, **13.** eggs, **14.** sandwich, **15.** sandwich, **16.** eggs
Page 110: 1. t, k, I fell and got a scratch on my knee. **2.** k, t, The workers knew how to patch the hole in the road. **3.** W, k, Wrap it in paper and tie it with a knot. **4.** k, w, Twist the knob on the door with your wrist. **5.** t, k, Never pitch a knife at anyone. **6.** k, w, Try not to knock the wrench off the bench. **7.** k, t, He will knit some socks and a

matching tie. **8.** t, w, They must watch the game and write a report.

Unit 6, Lesson 24

Page 112: 1. brown, **2.** yellow, **3.** green, **4.** blue, **5.** red, **6.** white, **7.** pink, **8.** gray, **9–10.** Answers will vary.
Page 113: 1. green, gray, **2.** gray, **3.** blue, **4.** yellow, **5.** pink, **6.** white, **7.** brown, **8.** red, **9.** pink, **10.** white, **11.** yellow, **12.** green, **13.** gray, **14.** blue, **15.** red, **16.** blue–brown, **17.** white, **18.** gray, **19.** brown, **20.** yellow
Page 114: 1. sh, ch, The huge ship moved through the sea. Nobody had to touch the wheel. **2.** ch, br, gr, I love fried chicken and potatoes with brown gravy. **3.** ch, sp, bl, Be sure to chew your food. Do not spill food on your blouse. **4.** th, ch, For dinner we ate a thick hamburger. I had a slice of cheese on mine. **5.** sh, ch, I hate to shave everyday. I often cut my chin with the blade.
Page 115: blue, white, brown

Unit 6 Review

Page 116: 1. how, **2.** green, **3.** soup, **4.** blue, **5.** bacon, **6.** cake, **7.** eggs, **8.** aunt, **9.** mother, **10.** where
Page 117: 11. white, **12.** grandmother, **13.** apple, **14.** daughter, **15.** sandwich, **16.** When, **17.** red, **18.** why, **19.** brown, **20.** what